Share Life's
Defining Moments

Eldon Weisheit

Share Life's Defining Moments

Relating to Your Grown Children

SAINT LOUIS

Copyright © 1997 Concordia Publishing House
3558 S. Jefferson Avenue, St. Louis, MO 63118-3968
Manufactured in the United States of America.

Library of Congress Cataloging-in-Publication Data

Weisheit, Eldon.
    Share life's defining moments : relating to your grown children /
Eldon Weisheit.
        p. cm.
    ISBN 0-570-04990-3
    1. Parent and adult child. 2. Empty nesters—Family relationships. 3. Intergen-erational relations. 4. Family—Religious aspects—Christianity. I. Title.
    HQ755.86.W45   1997
    306.874—dc21   97-8383

1   2   3   4   5   6   7   8   9   10   06   05   04   03   02   01   00   99   98   97

CONTENTS

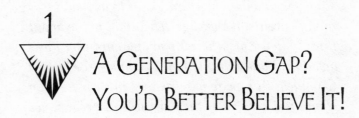

1
A GENERATION GAP?
YOU'D BETTER BELIEVE IT!

"I've had it with my kids. They are rude and thoughtless. They make too many demands on me and their father. They show no concern for our needs and our opinions, yet they expect us to be there to help them at the drop of a hat. They don't follow the way of living that we tried to teach them, then they blame us for everything that goes wrong in their lives."

This lament does not come from the overworked mother of elementary or high-school-age children. It's from the parent of children who have become adults in all relationships except the one with their parents. Some parents see it this way:

"When I grew up, I knew I was an adult when I left home. For me it was when I enlisted in the Navy. For some of my classmates it was when they got married, went to college, or got a job on their own. It was no big deal. We didn't need a big ceremony to show we could take care of ourselves. Our parents knew we were adults and we knew it.

"But it's not that way anymore. In one way my adult son and daughters are closer to us than I was to my parents at that age. They talk to me about things I never mentioned to my parents after I was an adult. Maybe they tell me too much—or I listen too much. But we're too involved in their lives on some subjects. Then they cut us out because we don't provide what they want."

Others who hear the frustrations of middle-age people talking about their adult sons and daughters recognize it as a simple problem—the generation gap. To a spectator it seems so simple: Of course, you have a different view of life than your children, no matter how old they are. They are in a different generation. They look at things in a different way.

That may be a diagnosis, but what's the prescription? Let's start with your view of the diagnosis. What is your picture of the generation gap?

- Is it the distance between two high walls—walls that the members of each generation hide behind to protect themselves from their ancestors on one side and their descendants on the other? Are the walls used to protect your generation from others and as a place to launch attacks against those who have gone before and those who will follow you? Are the walls something your children built to get away from you? Do they think you built the walls?

- Is the generation gap the measure of progress

between a generation and the one that follows? If there were no changes between generations, there would be no gap—and no progress. If great-grandparents and great-grandchildren lived in the same world, there would be no generation gap. That could happen only if someone pushed the "pause" button on the VCR called "life" and the entire world stopped.

- Is the generation gap both of the above? The generation gap is necessary for progress, but must the price include the physical and psychological warfare in the first description of the generation gap? Listen to the people of your generation when you get together. Isn't it true that you all talk about your children in one of two ways? You make your children sound like they have solved—or soon will solve—all the world's problems. They are the brightest and the best. Or they are the pits. They ignore you, depend on you for financial support, have bad friends, make bad decisions, and show other signs of incurable worthlessness. You panic at the thought that they will have to pay your Social Security.

When one of my sons was in that gray area between childhood and adulthood, he told me that he subtracted 25 percent from everything I said about him because as a father, I was not objective. I overrated him 25 percent when I praised him, and I underrated him 25 percent when I criticized him. He was right. That's part of our generation's contribution to the gap between us and our offspring.

Now imagine your sons and daughters talking with their own kind about you and other parents. How do they see you? Not only are they different, they see issues from a different point of view. The differences cannot be discussed from a common point of agreement because you see the situation from one side of the generation gap and they see it from the other.

The issue is not whether there is a generation gap because there is. But do the differences in generations have to be destructive? We also must ask if the gap could be a sign of progress. Ideally, the generation gap shows what happens when the younger generation learns from the older one and uses that knowledge to make a better life for themselves and the next generation. But not all change is progress. Some is regression. The energy spent on inter-generational warfare may prevent both generations from making a contribution to the world.

As a parish pastor, I spend a lot of time in premarital counseling with young couples between 25 and 32 years old. When they talk about themselves, they often describe their parents as controlling, rigid, self-centered people. At the wedding rehearsal I meet their parents and find them to be delightful, caring, loving people. Sometime between the beginning of the rehearsal dinner and the end of the wedding reception, the parents get around to asking me how this marriage will last because the bride or groom is so immature, self-centered, and unmotivated. And I had seen them as wonderful young people!

The war between the generations is a frequent subject for TV, movies, and books. Public figures face the possibility that an adult son or daughter will write a book describing every detail of their parent's personal failures. All the media attention indicates the generation gap has a high priority in the homes and on the phones of today's families.

Therefore, the purpose of this book is not to deny the existence of the generation gap but to recognize it and to make the best of it. Nor will this book attempt to solve the problems that exist between the generations. Those who strive after the blessings promised for peacemakers have learned long ago that one does not make peace by solving all problems but by helping people to live with one another peacefully, even when they have major differences.

Instead, the purpose of this book is to help the members of the older generation understand the responsibilities they have to the one that follows. This book will help people understand the problem before they try to solve it—or before they give up on it. It is addressed to the older generation because, no matter how much both sides deny it, they are still the ones in the position of authority. They always will see their sons and daughters as children, just as the younger generation will always see them as Mom and Dad.

The commandment regarding parents and children says: "Respect your father and your mother, as I, the LORD your God, command you, so that all may go well with you and so that you may live a long time in the land that I am giving you" (Deuteronomy 5:16). The promise in this commandment is not given to individuals. Then it would mean that those who respect their parents will live to an old age and those who are disrespectful will die young. That faulty interpretation has caused added grief for parents of children who die young—and it certainly cannot explain why some people live so long. Instead, the commandment is given to a community. The community where parents teach their children and children respect their parents will last a long time.

This commandment gives a promise to those involved in the battle between generations. To the parents, it promises that their values and faith can be transmitted through the next generation if they give what they have to give in a way that it can be used by those who follow. To the younger generation, who will become the older generation, this command promises that they may do new things and change the world for the better if they respect the values and faith of the generation from which they have received both problems and blessings. But the younger generation won't know that unless the older one shows them. That's you, Mom and Dad, no matter how old your children are.

Some Definitions

First, we need to identify the generations. At any given time, most families and communities are involved in only four generations. These generations will be identified as:

- *Generation A—the great-grandparents.* This generation is retired, elderly, and often has healed the problems. However, they are still a vital part of life and very definitely a part of the struggle among generations.

- *Generation B—the parents.* Although they were at one time the children of Generation A, these are the people who are perceived to be—and in some cases are—in charge. They are at a high level in their professional life, income, and sense of responsibility. They often feel that they are responsible for the other three generations (and sometimes they are). Generation B is the star of this book. If the issues discussed affect you, then you are the one who can do something about it.

- *Generation C—the sons and daughters of Generation B and the parents of Generation D.* These are the antagonists that thicken the plot of this book. Part of the problem of the generation gap is that our language does not provide a proper word for this generation in relationship to their parents. *Offspring* often seems out of place. *Heirs* has a legal and monetary tone. *Descendants* includes too many generations to be useful for this discussion. *Scion* is out of date. (I had to check the dictionary to be sure that it would be a proper word for Generation C. It is.) The people of this generation are not children, yet to identify them, we often call them the adult children of … . Personally, I am my mother's son, but I am not her child, and my former children are still my sons. Therefore, I will try to refer to Generation C as the sons and daughters of Generation B. But the phrase "adult children" will slip in.

Generation C is either coming up to bat or still playing in the first innings of life. They are mature enough to have seen the failures of Generation B, which are quite obvious to everyone (with the possible exception of those in Generation B). Some have decided to start fresh by forgetting everything that came from their ancestors. Others have given up because the problem is too great. Many members of Generation C recognize they are heading for their place in history and are struggling to do their best. By definition, this generation is the least focused as a group. They are like members of a football team during training camp. They each may have great abilities, but they have not yet had the opportunity to use those abilities as a team. Some of them don't even want to be on a team.

- *Generation D—the children of Generation C.* They are a part of the generation gap, not as combatants but as followers. A big part of the struggle among the other generations is about who will determine whom Generation D follows.

A member of Generation C says

"I don't want to have kids. I've figured out that the way my parents raised children was not right, and I won't repeat their mistakes. But I haven't figured out a better way to do it. At least I know better than to try."

A member of Generation B says

"I can see why my kids and their friends say they will never have any children. They have no values. They have a lot of ideas, but that's all it is— talk. I tell them that the real test of their opinion is for them to have children and take the risk of putting their talk into action."

The major conflict among the generations is between B and C. There seems to be a mutual support system between generations A and C and between generations B and D. It is easier for members of Generation C to accept advice from grandparents than from parents. It also is easier for grandparents to accept the differences they see in grandchildren than in their own children.

A member of Generation C says

"My parents never had time for me. They, especially Dad, were always busy with their own things. But now they have all this time for their grandchildren. They laugh and tell stories about what their grandchildren say and do, but they

17

*yelled and complained when I did the same things.
It ticks me off."*

Another definition of the generations: The noun *parent* has become the verb *to parent* for many people. Adults "parent" their children. Perhaps it is the conflict between the generations that has made many people realize that they need to learn to be a parent. So parenting classes are the "in" thing.

But how long do fathers and mothers parent their sons and daughters? It is obvious that infants need parenting. But as soon as they learn to walk on their own, they begin to show signs that they can get by with less parenting. However, the adults see what the children do when they want to make their own decisions—and the adults decide the children need more control. The increased control causes the children to increase their need for self-governance—and the stage is set for a lifetime of struggle about who is in charge. Often Generation C wants to get rid of parental authority while they are still really Generation D. Also, Generation B is often eager to give up their responsibilities before Generation C is ready to accept responsibility.

Many adults find that they are still parenting their adult sons and daughters—at least in parts of their lives. Sometimes it is difficult to know when the parenting should stop. That difficulty is not just a Generation B problem. Sometimes members of Generation C ask their parents for help in certain parts of their lives. However, they resent their parents when help is extended beyond the amount requested. Sometimes that is a thin, and a moveable, line.

The view from Generation C

"There are times when my parents could help me with a short-term loan, even though I am in my 30s. It's a business deal. But I won't ever ask again. Once was enough. They wanted to know every detail of my finances and they wanted to second-guess every decision I made about spending a buck."

The view from Generation B

"My daughter and her husband got into the habit of asking for money. We were glad to help them out. But I soon realized they were abusing our help. They'd go out to dinner and expensive restaurants and put it on a credit card. No worry: 'Mom and Dad will bail us out.' That's not a real world. We have learned to refuse their requests so they are forced to face reality."

When do mothers and fathers stop parenting? When do sons and daughters stop asking for it? The answers are not in the back of the book. However, all parts of the book will help adults who have adult sons and daughters. And all parts will help adults who have a mother and a father whom they cannot relate to as one adult to another. An important and treasured part of their relationship is that they have been parent and child. The experiences of the years when they lived as parents and children will always be a part of their relationship.

> *"My kids have lived on their own for 10 years. I can say this for them: They've never asked to move back to our home. I appreciate that, and I never want them to know what I'm telling you. But when they come back for a visit (vacation or something like that) and spend the night at our house, I never sleep well until I hear them come in and go to bed. I don't care what time my kids go to bed anymore! But I can't get out of the habit of listening if I know they are in my house. I guess it will always be that way."*

To complete our definitions: Just as parents need to know how to change their parenting methods as children grow older, children also need to redefine their response to their parents.

Note that the commandment about generations tells all generations to *respect* or honor their parents. That commandment applies to people of all ages.

Speaking to children, St. Paul tells them to obey their parents (Ephesians 6:1). Children respect their parents by obeying them. As they grow older, the need for respect remains, but the method will change. Both Generation B and Generation C must recognize that a change occurs in their relationship when obedience is no longer the issue. The change does not happen at a certain age or event. Both generations will recognize the change after it has occurred.

Understand Your Life's Orientation

Think of two people moving to a metropolitan area at the same time. One settles in a suburb and learns his way around the entire city from that one location. He gives directions to those who visit him according to the way he learned to see the city. He identifies the exit from the interstate, the shopping center, the name of his own suburb. He rarely, if ever, goes downtown.

Another person moves to the heart of the city. She learns her way around by bus, taxi, and walking. She identifies with tall buildings and government headquarters. When she has visitors, she directs them to parking places, ground transportation, and street corners. She rarely, if ever, goes to the suburbs.

Both people live in the same city. They may work together, go to church together, and share recreational activities. Both are affected by the same economic and political events. But each has a different orientation—a point of identity—in the same metropolitan area.

Each generation also has its own orientation. Even though generations B and C live in the same community (maybe even in the same house), even though they have a big overlap in many of their social, cultural, financial, and spiritual activities, they have a different orientation to what they see. Each generation sees all events from the places where they first experienced life.

First, consider your own orientation to life, no matter which generation is yours. Think about the way you learned about life. As a child you gradually became aware of what was going on around you. You learned by your own experience what family is, not because someone told you. You learned what home is and how one lives with others. You learned language, religion, music, art, entertainment, responsibilities, etc. No matter how long you live and how much you are able to grow beyond your childhood experiences, you always will understand yourself from the point of view where you first learned who you were.

> *"I remember how perfect things were when I was a child. My family went to church. Our grandparents, uncles, aunts, cousins were all there. I watched my uncles and father usher. Then we'd go to our grandparents for dinner. I thought that's how it would be when I grew up—but it's not. I'm only 23 years old and I feel lost already because I don't have a life like I expected. There have been three divorces and a death in my family. My husband and I live only five miles from where I grew up, but it seems like I am on a different continent."*

Your view of any person depends on how you first met that individual. For example, think of your doctor. If you met that person as a doctor, you will always see him or her in that role, even though you may see your doctor in church, social, or recreational activities. If one of your childhood friends grows up to be a doctor, you may have a difficult time accepting him or her as a professional because you still see the kid that you skipped school with. Can you put your life in his or her hands?

The people who lived in and around Nazareth had a difficult time accepting Jesus as the Messiah because they knew Him as a child. When He became famous (or infamous in the view of some), they kept reminding themselves that they knew His parents and His family. How can the kid you went skinny-dipping with be the Son of God?

However, others had a different view because they first met Jesus when He performed a miracle. They didn't think about His mother and father. They didn't remember the time He played in their backyard. Instead, they saw one who had the power to do miracles. While the people in His hometown could ignore Him, the religious leaders of Jerusalem took Him seriously because He had followers and the potential to take away their positions of power.

So generations B and C must have different views of each other by the very way they got acquainted.

Many a mother's first communication with her child was a kick through a stomach wall. Fathers and mothers began to identify with their child while it was still in the womb. Then they recall the details of birth—often recorded with pictures and video. They have many memories of things their children said and did, but the children do not remember. No matter how old their children become, parents will see something in them that no one else can ever see. A certain smile, a wave of a hand, a sound of the voice will cause a parent to see the child in a 40-year-old person.

Parents had a life before they had children. Parents know how their lives were changed by the birth and actions of their offspring.

Much of the generation gap is the result of parents still seeing their adult sons and daughters as children. Once people are completely mature, they may appreciate being "mothered" again. However, during the time (for some, it takes years) that children are turning into adults, they do not want to hear about all the cute and clever things they did as children. They don't want to be called by the pet names of childhood. They don't want to be reminded of the childish things they did.

Generation C, on the other hand, has a different view of their parents. They never knew what life was like without parents (or the surrogates who functioned as parents). They never had to be introduced to their parents. On their own, they figured out that the hairier one was a father and the softer one was a mother. Parents came as a part of the package called "life." Just as there was food, diapers, a bed, toys, and pets, there were parents. No big deal! Since their parents always have been a part of their lives, many young people assume that parents always will be there in the future. They refuse to even consider the possibility that their parents might get sick or die.

Much of the generation gap is caused because the younger generation takes the older one for granted. Parents have to put up with their children; they have to take care of them; they have to provide for them. "I didn't ask to be born" is the favorite line of a generation victim. "So who did?" is the response of Generation B.

Points of View

In the early '60s, I moved from the Midwest to a small town in southern Mississippi. I soon realized that I was in a totally different social, cultural, and spiritual environment than my previous orientation. The racial struggle was at its peak, but that was only a part of the differences between my view of life and the accepted community value system. In my effort to understand the differences, I often asked questions that began with, "You'll have to understand that I have a birth defect (I was born in Illinois), so I do not understand why ..." Amazingly, people understood my "birth defect" and were willing to explain why I saw things differently.

I ask you to use the same idea in your effort to understand the other generation. From your point of view, your orientation to life is correct. You are prepared to live in your time and your place according to the circumstances in which you were born. But the other generation (be it the one before you or the one after) has a birth defect. They do not understand how you look at life. They see things from a different point of view.

All of us think it would be rude (even more, it would be cruel) to blame a person for being born blind or with a club foot. That condition is a circumstance of the person's birth. Therefore, he or she is not morally or intellectually accountable for the disability. In the same way, you cannot blame your parents for being born a generation before you or your adult sons and daughters for being born a generation after you. From your point of view, that is their birth defect. Also be aware that, from their point of view, you have a birth defect.

Understand some of the reasons you and the other generation see life from different vistas.

- *Consider money.* I recently was involved in a discussion with three generations of the same family. I asked, "When you were in high school, what did it cost for you and a date to go to a movie and have a hamburger and Coke?" The person from Generation A said, "Two bucks." Generation B: "Five dollars." Generation C: "Twenty dollars." Generation C pays the same amount for a car that many members of Generation B paid for their first houses. Even though they all recognize that wages have increased with inflation, they still have different orientations on the value of the dollar.

"My son lives in Mexico City and must deal

with the differences between dollars and pesos and slow mail. So he has his bills that are paid in dollars sent to my address. Even though I pay his bills with his money, I need to check his credit card statements as I check my own. I know it is none of my business where he buys his clothes and how much he spends, but circumstances force me to know. Telling this story may help me keep my resolve not to give him financial advice."

Add to this the fact that Generation B grew up with a bigger need (inherited from Generation A) to save for the rainy day, to avoid going into debt, and to pay one's own way. Application: Accept the fact that Generation B thinks their adult sons and daughters have a birth defect because they do not know how to handle money. Accept the fact that Generation C thinks their parents have a birth defect that makes them cheap.

- *Examine the language that people use to express themselves.* The older members of Generation B grew up with the shock of hearing Rhett Butler say, "Frankly, my dear, I don't give a damn." in "Gone With the Wind." With their own eyes they saw the same word when they read *The Man without a Country* when Philip Nolan said, "I do not give a damn about the United States." Believe it or not, that was pretty heady stuff 50 years ago. It wasn't that people in Generation B did not know and use the forbidden word. The difference is that it was not publicly acceptable.

Compare that with the acceptable language of today. Few words are shocking, and few words are forbidden. Those that are on the remaining "no-no" list can easily be communicated by omissions and first letters. Generation B grew up saying they had to get their act together and that they were ticked off. Only in the '60s for the first expression and the '80s for the second did these ideas become connected with bodily eliminations.

Even though members of Generation B have learned the new expressions, they still react to them with more emotion. They think the younger generation has a birth defect in the way they speak with open vulgarity. On the other hand being "up-tight" is a birth defect of Generation B from the point of view of their adult sons and daughters.

- *Understand why the two generations may have far different views on family.* Some of the members of Generation B grew up without knowing anyone who was divorced. Many did not have a divorce in their own family. However, the younger generation may have a hard time thinking of anyone who does not have a divorce in their family.

"My husband and I went to a nice restaurant to celebrate our 37th wedding anniversary. We

told the maitre d' about our special day. Soon bus-
boys and kitchen employees were coming out to
congratulate us—or just to look at us. Several told
us that they didn't know anyone who had been
married for 37 years."

This does not mean that Generation B marriages have not ended in divorce. Their generation has become the first to have a high divorce rate. Yet their attitude about divorce comes from their childhood orientation toward marriage. Members of Generation C may be more open to the possibility of divorce because it has been a common occurrence among the people they know. On the other hand, many younger people are being more cautious about marriage because they have personally experienced the tragedy of divorce in their own childhoods.

The two generations may have many other different orientations about marriage. The older generation has experienced (or been told about) more family togetherness. They know what it is like to have uncles, aunts, and a great variety of degrees of cousins—all within visiting range. Many people in the younger generation have no feeling about a "home place."

A member of Generation C says

"I don't know what to say when people ask me
where I'm from. I lived for only a few months in the
state where I was born while my father finished on-

the-job training. I went to four different schools in three different states. I feel like I am from 'over there' someplace."

A member of Generation B says

"When I grew up, everyone I met knew my family. I thought I would get out of the loop one time when I dated a girl who lived two small towns away. However, her father asked me, 'Are you Wilson's grandson?' I was."

The parents who grew up in one community (and have since become nomadic) still have a far different orientation to their roots than the generation that started on the road.

- *Realize how the generations have a different view of national leaders and other public figures.* Generation B remembers (or has heard about) their president who spent most of his term in a wheelchair, but they didn't know it because the media didn't reveal the big secret. Generation B lives at a time when they know the kind of underwear their president wears because he told them. This difference is not just between the personalities of two presidents. It is evidence of the different attitude about a leader's private life, about the media's responsibility, and (I guess) a different attitude about underwear.

The older generation saw movie stars, sports figures, and others as heroes whose lives were examples of how to live. Many of their images of public figures later turned out to be false (leading to a cynical attitude by another generation), but people in Generation B still live with memories of heroes on pedestals. That is their birth defect. Meanwhile, Generation C has a different birth defect. They have anti-heroes and follow the example of those who destroy their lives with drugs, alcohol, violence, and sexual deviations.

Generation B went along with the pretense that "Leave It to Beaver" was the way American families lived. The next generation gagged at the thought. They wanted honesty.

A member of Generation B said, "If you want to really know about marriage and family, watch, 'Married with Children' and 'Roseanne.' " So I did. Both TV programs are just as unreal as "Leave It to Beaver," only they are on the other end of the spectrum. Instead of pretending to be too good, they pretend to be too bad.

No marriage could survive with husbands and wives, parents and children, brothers and sisters treating each other as they do on the modern programs about marriage. Just as drunks may be fun on stage but tragic in real life, families that verbally abuse one another and degrade work, sexuality, school, and almost everything else cannot provide an example of what a family is supposed to be. Both generations grew up with a birth defect from their views of family on TV.

A Title for Each Generation

History develops a name for most generations. The people of the '20s were the Flappers. Those born in the '30s (this includes me) are the Silent Generation. (It looks as though there may never be a U.S. president who was born during that decade.) In more current times, we have had the Flower Children and the Hippies and the Boomers. We have a decade of greed. Some are calling the present crop the Angry Generation. Life is now so uncertain that the next crop is called Generation X.

The titles come from overall impressions and certainly do not represent all the people included in each category. However, all people of a generation are affected by the social mores of their time. When Emily Post directed the manners of society, she told us how to treat servants and where to leave calling cards. Miss Manners, the present high priestess of social behavior, tells us how to include unmarried couples who live together in our social events and when blue jeans are appropriate. By the way, Miss Manners says we now have the first generation of parents (Generation B) who are uncomfortable asking their children (Generation C) to social events. They also are the first parents afraid to invite themselves to their adult sons' or daughters' homes.

Those who study social development also say that the present Generation C is the first group that does not expect to be more financially and socially successful than their parents. In all previous generations, parents and children expected the younger generation to do better than the one before. The older generation regarded it as a part of their success when they saw their adult children outshine them.

That idea may be depressing to Generation C, but the flip side is that their generation will be the first to inherit large sums of money. Large family inheritances used to be limited to the rich. But wealth is more evenly distributed now, and many more people will inherit more than the old family home and lots of pictures.

The promise of a larger inheritance for the present Generation C isn't all good news. Generation B is going to live longer than all previous generations because most of them have had better health care and health habits. As a result, Generation C may inherit lots of money—but not for a long time.

Generation B: It's Your Move

You love your children, no matter how old they are, no matter what they have done or not done. Do not expect them to love you in the same way you love them. Compare how you feel about your parents with how you feel about your children. Love always flows downhill in the generation game. It should be that way. Maybe this book will help you gain a better understanding of your adult sons and daughters. Maybe it will help you to help them gain a better understanding of you.

2

From Changing of the Diapers to Changing of the Guard

Maybe you've heard this story:

A mother called to her son and told him to get out of bed. He ignored her. She continued to yell at him and finally said, "You have to get up and get ready for church right now!"

The son replied, "Give me two good reasons why I have to."

"First of all," his mother said, "you are 35 years old. And second, you're the pastor."

This story introduces two questions. First, *when does parenthood start?* The answer is *not* when a baby is born. All who have been through the process recognize that nine months provide about the right time to get used to the idea of parenthood. For many people those nine months are a good time to take a crash course in remedial maturity. Now is the time to get ready for the responsibility of caring for a child. However, many people start their education for parenthood long before conception takes place. While the possibility of a baby is still a glint in the eye of many wanna-be parents, they start the process toward becoming a mother or father.

All the talk about when parenthood starts is a philosophical look at the past. However, becoming a parent is not a once-in-a-lifetime experience. It is a total change in your identity. You have become a mother or a father.

That brings us to the second question: *When will parenthood end?* This chapter examines the question from several points of view. For the moment let's skip to the chase and give the answer: Never. Parenthood, like marriage, is an until-death-do-you-part relationship. Notice that the question was not, "When does childhood end?" There is an end to the time when a person is a child, but as an adult, each person still has parents or memories of parents. That's part of the blessings of life—and it's part of the struggles of life.

The goal is not to determine when childhood ends so a legal or moral end of parental responsibility can be established. Rather, the goal is to find a way for the two generations to accept the continual changes as parents and children grow through the levels described as generations D, C, B, and A. A lot happens between the time of the changing of the diapers and the changing of the guard when the younger generation becomes self-supporting and self-governing. As those changes are made, the relationship between parents and children adjusts to the new situations. When those adjustments are made at a gradual and acceptable rate to both generations, the transitions are smooth. Sometimes circumstances force a sudden adjustment and the relationship will have to survive a rapid change. In other cases, the relationship may remain at a level that is no longer appropriate. Then an explosion in the relationship will be necessary to free both generations from the status quo.

When Does Generation D Become Generation C?

When do children become adults? As parents, you answer that question differently than your sons and daughters. Though it is out of the range of this book, the arena for the struggles between parents and adult sons and daughters starts in the teenage years when … (We must now give two points of view.)

> *Teenager:* "One minute they tell me to stop acting like a child and the next minute they tell me to wipe my nose or say 'please.' They seem to want me to be an adult when it fits their needs yet want me to be a kid when they feel a need to be in control again."

> *Parent:* "They want to make their own decisions about school, money, friends, and other things. But when we let them make their own choices, they goof up. The schoolwork doesn't get done. They spend money on all kinds of things that aren't necessary, then they come back to us and expect us to bail them out by paying for the things

*that are necessary. They want to be adults so they
can do what they want, but they still want us to
take the responsibility for their bad decisions."*

This struggle is acceptable, and probably even
necessary, between parents and teenagers. But it is
destructive if the struggle is still going on when the
sons and daughters are in their 20s. In today's world
it's sometimes still going on when the younger generation is above 30.

When do children become adults? A legal
answer named an age: 18 or 21. There are symbolic
answers too. The Bible says that a "man leaves his
father and mother and is united with his wife, and
they become one" (Genesis 2:24). Marriage is one
sign that the child has become an adult. But marriage
doesn't always guarantee maturity. Others who don't
get married do become adults.

Graduation from high school was my clue that it
was time to hit the road under my own direction. In
today's world the sign would more likely be graduation from college, trade school, or (the one parents
love) to a job that has paydays.

At one time puberty was a sign of maturity, but
that day is long past. Primitive cultures had a variety
of rituals that showed the child had become an adult.
Living alone in the outback did it for the aborigines
of Australia. Killing a bear or building a cabin did it
for some frontier American men. A Bar or Bat Mitz-
vah was a stepping stone to adulthood for a Jewish
child just as confirmation also became one for many

38

Christian families. In the secular world a driver's license is a symbol of making a big step toward adulthood. (I know one woman who said she realized she was an adult when she had to buy her own toilet paper.)

When my childhood family drove home from my paternal grandmother's funeral, I remember my mother saying, "I am now the oldest Mrs. Weisheit." Thirty years later I figured out that she was 27 at the time. Her parents had both been dead for several years.

Everyone needs some proof of maturity. The complication is that proof of maturity for Generation C will not always satisfy Generation B. Besides, the climb from childhood to adulthood is not one long hill. Instead it is a series of hills and valleys so the trip involves ups and downs (with more of the first).

"One of my co-workers was in his mid-20s— 15 years younger than I am. I thought he was extremely mature, and we became good friends. When his parents came to town, we invited them and my young friend to our home for dinner. I was shocked at my friend's change of attitude. When his parents were around, he acted like a teenager. The polite person became rude; the open person became defensive. When his parents left town, he returned to adulthood."

The uphill road to maturity also has more than one lane. One may be very mature on the job and a pre-adolescent at home. One may be very mature as coach of the Little League team (that's the one in charge) and of no use whatever as a member of another athletic team (that's the one who must follow the direction of others). Some can be very mature when all is going well but fall apart when something unexpected or tragic happens. Equally true, some may be irresponsible on the normal days but come through in an emergency with strong leadership and maturity.

> *"I had a friend who by his mid-30s had all the signs of success. He was a city judge, had a beautiful home, and had been married for 10 years. His wife developed an illness that meant she would die in a few months. They both regretted their decision to put off having children, but he explained, 'I wasn't mature enough to have a dog until three years ago.' "*

Children become adults when they accept responsibility for their own lives. In some cases they do not want that responsibility. Some people in their 20s, 30s, and even older prefer to stay in a childlike relationship with their parents. Part of the problem may be that they want someone to provide the necessities of life for them. A bigger part of the problem is that they may want someone to blame for anything that goes wrong.

> *"Our son, a 30-year-old college graduate, moved back into our home after we had moved to*

another state. He drank my beer, used my postage
stamps, and acted like we owed it to him. Then we
discovered that he was telling our friends that he
was giving up his own career to help care for us
because his mother was ill and I had an alcohol
problem. With that, he was out of the house! We've
done well for 10 years without him; I wish I could
say the same for our son."

Members of Generation B who feel that their
adult sons or daughters are not mature need to face
reality. Which is the best question: "Does our son or
daughter refuse to grow up?" or "Is our son or
daughter capable of growing up?"

Those same sons and daughters may ask the
questions this way: "Why don't my parents recognize
that I am an adult?" or "Why won't they accept me as
I am rather than expect me to be what they think I
should be?"

When Do Parents Give Up Authority?

Generation B looks at it this way: "When will they
ever grow up and become responsible for themselves?"

Generation C has a different view: "When will
they recognize that I grew up a long time ago? I don't
need their supervision anymore."

While it is true that parents cannot give their
children maturity, it is also true that parents must
give up control of their children.

No one would argue that parents have total
responsibility for a 5-year-old child. Because they

have the responsibility for the child, they also have authority over the child. Authority and responsibility are twins. You can't have one without the other. In the climb toward maturity, children must accept more responsibility to have authority over their lives. At the same time the parents must give up their authority over their children so their children can accept the responsibility. This transfer of authority and responsibility from one generation to the next is a long process. It starts in early childhood and continues until ...

> "In our family it was real easy for the kids to know when they would be treated like adults. From early on, we let them know we would treat them that way when they acted that way. If they made a decision, they paid for it—money or otherwise. The same was true if their father or I made the decision. There were some ups and downs, but they are all responsible adults now."

This book will not give a date or an event when the guard changes between generations B and C, but it will insist that the change must be made—by both generations.

Some mothers and fathers are overly eager to get rid of the responsibilities of parenthood. It was fun to have little children, but teenagers are a pain—get them out of here! Boarding schools are filled with older children whose parents would rather pay someone else to put up with their offspring. At one time the military was the place where a sergeant replaced Mom and Dad. Force children to become independent too early and you may make them very dependent later in life. Premature independence may destroy the adult relationship between generations B and C.

Other parents cannot face their children's need to become independent. They enjoy having their children around. They like to hear the stories their sons and daughters tell. They enjoy their friends. They want to put time on hold and year after year recycle the experience of being parent and child.

When it comes time for the high school graduate to go to college, some parents say it would save money for the son or daughter to live at home. Then when the college graduate applies for work, some parents encourage him or her to still live at home "until you get your feet on the ground."

Many parents make offers that are difficult for young adults to refuse. Generation C asks: "Why live in a lonely apartment with old furniture when I could live in comfort in my parents' home? Why eat my own cooking or fast food when Mom doesn't mind fixing a little extra? Why use my own quarters to do laundry when I can use my parents' washer and drier? (Maybe Mom will even do the work and throw in ironing at no extra cost.)"

It sounds like a good deal for Generation C, but is it Generation B's way of maintaining control? There may be no financial charge for room and board (at least not a realistic amount), but Generation C may pay a high-priced mortgage on their own maturity.

"When we got married I loved my in-laws. They were fun to be with, so they became our best friends. They went to ball games and dinner with us. They gave us the money to buy a house—four doors away from their own. Her father did our yard work; her mother cleaned our house. It took a year for me to figure out that my wife's parents owned us. They still own her—but not me. We are divorced."

Few parents plan to control the lives of their adult sons and daughters. They don't intend to keep them in a childlike relationship in their adult years. What happens is that they extend childhood a few months at a time. They may even complain to friends and other family members about their "children" still living at home. The complaining explains that it is still necessary for them to care for their children. Then one year the parents realize that something is wrong. The pattern that was meant to be "for another six months" has become a way of life.

"I have a great adult relationship with my parents, but my older sisters still have conflicts with them. I finally figured out why. My older sisters have never lived with or near our parents since they were adults. They still react to Mom and Dad as they did when they last lived together—in their high school years. I left home at the same time, but I came back

and lived with my parents. We became adult friends.
Now I live nearby and we enjoy one another."

Who Makes the Change?

In some families the transfer of authority and responsibility from Generation B to C seems as easy as one member of a relay team passing the baton to another. They are on the same team and know how to work together.

In other families the transfer of power could be better pictured as a civil war. Members of Generation C are not content to pack up their lives and leave. Instead, they want to take over the lives of their parents in a revolt against the existing regime. Or Generation B is like Pharaoh of ancient Egypt and will not let Generation C go. In this scenario parents battle to keep control of the kids.

Who is responsible for changing the guard? Is it the parents' job to kick the children out of the nest? Is it the younger generation's job to assume self-responsibility?

Unlike many questions in this book, there is an answer to those in the previous paragraph. The answer is simple: The one who complains about the situation is the one who must make the change.

In many cases members of Generation B will complain that their adult sons and daughters are taking advantage of them. The adult children still expect financial help from their parents. They expect the parents to buy cars, pay for vacations, and take care of grandchildren. One of the chief agenda items at a Generation B gathering is how they are giving up the best years of their lives for their adult offspring. They can't do the traveling they had planned or build the dream house they had talked about because they are still supporting their children. They are the victims in their minds. In reality they are responsible for allowing their adult sons and daughters to remain unweaned.

Now listen to Generation C when they gather at their watering holes. They say their parents still want to control their lives. Their parents want to tell them which car or house to buy, which job to take. Generation C complains because their parents are spoiling their children, interfering in their marriage, and (get ready for this) *treating them like children.* They are victims of their parents. They complain that their parents don't treat them like adults, but they let it continue because they don't want to lose what they get out of the relationship—generally financial support or the handy excuse that someone else is the cause of their failures.

If these negative descriptions of generations C and B are true of both parties, the unhealthy relationship and the complaining will continue for years. Their codependence is damaging their lives, but it is easier for them to maintain it than to make the effort to change the relationship.

However, if only one of the generations wants to maintain the civil war, the other one can end it. The movie "War Games," which was an afterthought of the Cold War, ended with this solution: "The only way not to lose the game is not to play the game." If both generations feel the need to win, the inter-generational skirmishes will continue. It would be destructive to the family if one generation was defeated or surrendered, so the struggle goes on. But if the mature generation (that does not always mean the older one) stops playing, the war is over. No one wins! No one loses!

> *"I grew up with an abusive father who could not show emotion. It was a problem for me, but I found freedom because my husband was a kind, loving, noncontrolling person. However, the old memories of my father came back when my daughter became engaged. I was afraid that her new husband would be like my father. It took a lot of work on my part, and some outside help, to see that my future son-in-law was like my husband, not my father."*

To stop playing the game of parent- and child-bashing does not mean that the generations need to divorce each other. Instead, they need to define their adult relationship so it includes the areas that they can enjoy together. The subject that causes conflict must be removed from the family agenda.

In all our social encounters, we learn to avoid the subjects that will cause conflict. You don't talk politics with certain people. You don't talk about religion with others. You don't serve alcohol to some of your friends. With others you avoid the subject of race, the

47

kind of car you drive, and other topics that some people are allergic to. Many parents and adult sons and daughters need to develop the same courtesy for one another. Arguing about your opinions will not change the other generation. If you keep quiet about the subject, they may let their guard down and find someone else who can help them make the changes that could be necessary in their lives.

Each of the remaining chapters of this book is about a subject that may be part of the "changing of the guard" experience. No one will make the change for you, but these chapters may help you and the other generations define yourselves for one another.

3

WHOSE IS THE STATUS AND THE POWER AND THE MONEY?

Is the rivalry between parents and their adult sons and daughters a part of the system? Is the conflict between the generations the result of sin because it divides parents and children and hinders progress of the human race? Or is the struggle a necessary part of relationships as parents need to release their children and children need to advance beyond the achievements of their parents? Or is it all the above?

The phenomenon occurs so often that it cannot be regarded as a random personality conflict. Philosophy and psychology both include the premise of a conflict between father and son, between mother and daughter. Consider a partial list of inter-generational struggles in the Bible:

- Noah and Ham
- Abraham and Lot (uncle and nephew)
- Isaac and Jacob
- Rebecca and Esau

- Laban and Jacob (father-in-law and son-in-law)
- Jacob and most of his sons
- Eli and Hophni and Phinehas
- Saul and Jonathan
- David and Amnon
- David and Absalom
- The waiting father and the prodigal son

Apparently Joseph and Jesus got along fine, but that shows the advantage of having an earthly father who is willing to listen to angels and a son who is the Son of God.

Talk shows and newspapers are filled with conflict between parents and their adult sons and daughters. Rob Reiner, a top name in show biz, talks about the problem of having a father, Carl Reiner, in the same business. The son remembers the success of his father and that's enough to make it a burden for him. The conflict between two leading news reporters—the father and son nonteam of Mike and Chris Wallace—is well known. *Mommy Dearest*, the book by Joan Crawford's daughter, has provided the outline for less sensational, but still very painful, conflicts between generations. The list of public battles between the generations also includes Prince Charles of England and his father, Prince Philip.

If biblical families, royal families, and well-known entertainment families engage in inter-generational battles, is it only a problem of the rich and famous? Or does that set an example for the rest of us? Or is it more evidence that there is no difference between the famous and the commonplace? The conflict between the generations is just a normal part of life.

The list of public conflicts between parents and their adult sons and daughters could be matched by another list of great partnerships between generations B and C. The names on farm trucks and many businesses often include "and Sons." The public testimony of many adults includes praise and appreciation for parents and for adult sons and daughters. Those relationships were not as perfect in private as in public, but the majority has both generations being able to cope with the inadequacies of the other and to maintain a loving and enduring relationship.

In reality, few inter-generational relationships are as bad as the model of *Mommy Dearest* or as good as the testimonies at weddings, anniversaries, and funerals. Most relationships between generations B and C are stressful at times and comfortable and fulfilling at other times. Those who want to improve their ability to get along with adult sons and daughters can learn from the extremely bad examples of those who have major problems and from the extremely good examples of those who have it all (or at least most of it) together.

If you are a member of a generation B and C team that gets along, count your blessings and enjoy your relationship. But do not condemn others who don't enjoy a similar relationship.

*"I am uncomfortable when I visit my sister
because I want to talk about my son and his success in his work. I want to show pictures of my
grandchildren and tell about what they say and do.
But my sister hasn't heard from her daughter for
three years, and her son only shows up when he
wants money. I know I was not a better mother
than my sister was. But how can I tell her that?"*

If you are part of the warfare between generations B and C, do not try to pretend that all is well
between you and your adult sons and daughters—or
between you and your parents. Do not envy what
appears to be perfect relationships between other
adults and their parents—it will only increase the
stress in your own family. Instead, try to understand
the differences that cause conflict in your family.

Understanding and admitting the differences is
the first step for improved relationships. It does not
mean that you must achieve a picture-perfect family,
but you can make the most of what you have. This
book is not a solution but a way to help you deal with
the situation. The comment that "dysfunctional family" is redundant is not a negative view of life. It only
recognizes that sin has made us all dysfunctional in
relationships. As Christians we can confess the sin,
accept the forgiveness, and get on with life.

*"My counselor told me that I had to accept the
fact that I would not have a close relationship with
my adult daughters for the rest of my life. He said*

I had to recognize that I might never be a grand-mother—and if it did happen, I would not have the relationships with my grandchildren that I wanted. I thought that the day I accepted those facts would be the saddest day of my life, but it wasn't. Instead it was like a new beginning. I starting living the other parts of my life. I volunteer in the church day care center, and I have a great time with other people's grandchildren."

"Yes," Jesus said to them, "and I tell you that anyone who leaves home or brothers or sisters or mother or father or children or fields for Me and for the gospel, will receive much more in this present age. He will receive a hundred times more houses, brothers, sisters, mothers, children, and fields—and persecutions as well; and in the age to come he will receive eternal life." (Mark 10:29–30)

One more *if*. If you have a good relationship with one of your adult sons or daughters but not with another, you have a special problem. Do not let the good relationship with one make you feel guilty about the difficult relationship with the other. Do not let the problem with one take away the joy of your relationship with the other.

"Our family has a good time when we are together for holidays and special occasions, even though one daughter is never there. We don't pretend that she can't be there. She doesn't want to be with

us. It's strange, but she has helped me understand God's grace even more. I love all my children, including the one that doesn't share her life with us. But I pray for her even more than I pray for the others."

The boys grew up, and Esau became a skilled hunter, a man who loved the outdoors, but Jacob was a quiet man who stayed at home. Isaac preferred Esau, because he enjoyed eating the animals Esau killed, but Rebecca preferred Jacob. (Genesis 25:27–28)

Is the Conflict over Power?

Is every son a prince waiting to become king ... every daughter a princess waiting to become queen? Do parents teach their young children to be like themselves only to become afraid of the competition when the children become adults? Do children choose their parents as models for life, then blame the model if things turn out wrong?

"I watch the conflict between my husband and our son and it breaks my heart because they are exactly alike. Maybe that's why it is so easy for me to love them both. Yet I wonder if either of them likes himself because each seems to dislike his own qualities in the other. Don't let them know I said this because if they thought I said they were alike, they'd both be angry about it."

In the days when sons followed in their father's footsteps and when mothers oversaw family clans, there could be conflict for control. The sons wanted to operate the family farm or business the way they thought it should be done. The father wanted to keep a good thing going. Daughters combined the careers of home and work and wanted to do better than their mothers, who had only one job. Mothers were sure that their way was best for the family.

But the rivalry between generations is more than people competing to climb the same ladder to success. The conflict can exist in families where the two generations are in totally different careers. In many cases, the conflict can be defined in simple terms. One is that Generation B will not give up control of their adult sons and daughters. They "know better" than their children, and it will always be that way. The conflict is complete when Generation C bases their success, their self-esteem, on a need to do things better than their parents. If they can't do more, they can still "win" by putting their parents down.

"My parents made it very clear that if I wanted to go to college at their expense, they would choose the school and my career field. Since they were paying for my education, they felt they had the right to make the decisions."

"Our son has a good, honest job and provides for his family. It involves manual labor and he gets dirty every day. His job is fine with us, but he can't

accept that. He has to tell the relatives that he has
a 'real job' because he doesn't sit around in an office
wearing a necktie like his father. We wish that he
could feel good about his job as it is and accept the
fact that we are happy about his work. But he can't
and he makes us feel that we are at fault."

Notice how this struggle for the driver's seat is a natural part of childhood and adolescence. As I worked on this manuscript, my 4-year-old grandson visited me and said, "Today I am the daddy, and you are my little boy." We did it and had a great time because he was in charge. Children need to play as a way of practicing for adulthood. However, letting a child play at being in charge is a lot different for the parent than having an adult child actually in charge. It also is much easier to play at being in charge than it is to be responsible. It's also easier to play the game with a grandchild than with a child.

Teenagers measure their progress by comparing themselves to parents. Boys feel a need to be as tall, or taller, than their father. Girls need to develop a figure like, or better than, their mothers. They watch for these signs so they will know they are on the right track toward maturity.

All this is necessary and good for children and teenagers, but it is destructive when the competition for power is still a part of the relationship between parents and their adult sons and daughters.

"Our daughter's husband was the perfect son-

in-law. No family could have been closer. Now we hardly speak to one another. The trouble came when we became business partners instead of in-laws. We thought that we got along so well as family that we would be perfect in business together. But it didn't work."

Rather than see the struggle for power between the generations as a part of normal competition in the marketplace, let's reverse the view. The competition for power is a natural struggle between the generations and is sometimes played out in the area of vocation.

From the perspective of Generation B

The desire to reproduce one's own kind is a natural part of animal and human life. When God finished His six days of creation, He could rest because He had built the continuing power of creation into His first models. God's first commandment to the human race (and the only one we've kept) was to be fruitful and multiply (Genesis 1:28). The desire to have children was a part of God's creation. The ability to reproduce was included when He said that He was pleased with what He had created (Genesis 1:31). God inspected all that He had done, and He knew it would work.

However, God also built freedom of will into the humans in His system. We were made in His image; therefore, like God, we had the freedom to love and serve both God and other people, but we were not forced to do it. When our first ancestors sinned, that sin became a factor in all our decisions and all our desires. Sin and its results became a part of our genetic code.

The good desire to have children also was affected by the factor of sin. This does not mean it became sinful to want to have children. Rather, it means that sin affected the holy desire for the gift of children from God. By eating from the tree of the knowledge of good and evil, Adam and Eve remodeled God's creation to make their will opposed to the will of God. This does not mean that their actions were now divided into the good (because they still had the knowledge of good) and evil (because they had added that knowledge to their existence). Instead, it means that they mingled human evil with the goodness of God. When we do good things, there is still a minority element in us that adds some evil to the good. When we do evil things, there is still a minority element in us that makes us feel guilty and wish we had done better. Isaiah explains it, "All of us have been sinful; even our best actions are filthy through and through" (Isaiah 64:6).

Even the best desire to be fruitful and to multiply became another expression of human sinfulness. Yet it also remained a holy desire given by God.

One way that sin sneaks into the reproductive process is when the desire to have children becomes a desire to own them. Sin makes parents see the conception and birth of children as an opportunity to be a god. Just as *the* God made human beings, so can they. Just as *the* God could tell His creation what to do, so can they. Just as *the* God made humans in His own image, so can they.

> *"When I accepted the fact that my 21-year-old son was very angry at me, I searched to find the reason. One thing that I remembered: When he was a child, we had a routine that I regarded as a game. I would say, "You are my little boy." He would say, "No, I'm not." I would say, "Yes, you are, and I have a birth certificate that says you belong to me." Now I realize that it was not a good game for him. I know I don't own him now and that I never did. We had a hard time talking, so I wrote him a letter and apologized to him about the game. He never mentioned the letter, but our relationship improved."*

Sin can contaminate the holy desire to have children in many ways. Before Social Security and retirement plans, parents knew they needed children to provide for them when they were old. When families lived on farms or had their own small businesses, more children (especially males) meant more workers. A boy-child added more to the parents' security than a girl-child. Human greed infested the holy desire to have children.

Sometimes parents want children so they can have clones of themselves. Unlike God, these self-appointed gods do not give children free will. If they provide for their children as God provides for His, these parents think they will get the dividends of controlling their own creation. Parents (and grandparents) of babies and young children want the credit for their offspring's wit, appearance, and intelligence. However, if they claim credit for the good, they must later take responsibility for what they see as bad in their descendants. In these cases, parents become aware that they are losing control as their children grow older. If they feel their children's faults reflect on themselves, they will try to reach out and regain, or even tighten, the control. They still need to control their children to protect their own reputation.

A member of Generation C says:

> "My mother has tried to control every detail in my life. When I make a decision that is good, she gets the credit. When I make a bad decision, she says, 'You should have listened to me.' She is a nurse, and when I decided to get a degree in nursing, it was a confirmation of her good influence on me—though from my point of view she had nothing to do with it. She even announced that she would quit her job and go back to school with me to get her master's degree. I have just applied to a school four states away—one that does not offer a master's degree in nursing."

There's one danger of a parent's need to control adult sons or daughters: The more the control is threatened, the stronger it becomes. Both generations include the control factor as they adopt their methods of dealing with issues in the relationship. Therefore, if either tries to change, it also changes the rules of the family relationship—and neither generation can break free from the problem of control.

> *"I have accepted the fact that I was and that I am a controlling person. I raised my kids that way. They tried to tell me, and I wouldn't listen. My husband tried to tell me, and I wouldn't listen. So I went to a counselor. She made me hear it. Now I agree! They were all right about me. Now I want out of it. I don't want to control them. I want them to have their own lives. But guess what—they won't let me. They keep putting me in the place that makes me responsible for everything they do. I can see what they are doing. They have a way to blame me for all their mistakes. They even say it's my fault they think that way."*

Sometimes parents who discover that they are still controlling their adult sons and daughters feel that they have only one way out of the situation— end the relationship entirely. They may think they have to divorce their children by declaring themselves failures as parents and denying all responsibility for their offspring. The relationship must change, but it need not be that drastic. The parents may have to restrict their involvement in the lives of their sons and daughters. They may have to avoid certain topics. They may have to refrain from giving advice and help—even when their sons and daughters ask for it.

> *"I have a widowed friend who tells people she*

has no children. She is a very strong, controlling person and has caused problems in the church where I met her. When her sister visited, I accidentally discovered that she had a son. The conflict between the two became so great when he was in his early 20s that she denies that he exists."

In most conflicts the person who has the perceived position of authority must be the first to reach out to the other. Note the emphasis on the "perceived." From the parents' point of view, they may have no authority left. But if the adult sons and daughters still live with an image of parental authority, the perception is still there. The resolution cannot come from a judgment of who is right and who is wrong. That is no longer the issue. The issue is (as seen from the position of Generation B) that the parent still wants a relationship with the adult children. Therefore, the parent can reach out to the younger generation by looking for areas of involvement that do not involve authority.

Parents and adult sons and daughters who have a history of conflict over authority need not end their relationship—but they must redefine it. They must establish areas of their lives that they can share and enjoy without bringing up the problems of control. They need to search for, and find, the good things that were part of their experiences when the members of Generation C were children. They need to find new points of interest that they can share as equal adults. Most of all, they need to recognize that the relationship cannot be, and need not be, perfect. (The desire for a perfect relationship may well be a big part of the problem.) Now they need to look forward to and enjoy whatever events they can share with their adult sons and daughters.

To Generation B: Do not be a victim of your adult sons and daughters. You are hurting them as well as yourself if you continue in patterns that cause anger and frustration in everyone. To help you do this, look at the same situations from their point of view.

From the perspective of Generation C

Babies are born totally dependent on their parents. From the infant's point of view, that's the way it is supposed to be. Babies have no doubt that someone is going to provide for them if they yell loud enough, and they have no feeling that they must return the kindness that they receive. Being dependent is the way to go!

It is natural for babies to see their parents as a stand-in for God or as God Himself. Unaware of the distinction, the parents serve as a god because they have done the creating and the providing—both important parts of God's job description.

Because parents have total responsibility for a baby, they also have total authority over the child born to them. They give the child a name and decide what language it will speak, what clothes it will wear, what food it will eat, where it will live, what religion it will have, and what health care it will receive. Because the parents have the responsibility, they also have the authority. Being in charge is the way to go!

This is a good deal for babies who have no ability to provide for themselves—like living in the Garden of Eden. But as babies grow older, they begin to wonder why parents get to make all the decisions. Why do I have to eat peas when I like cookies better? Why do I have to take a nap when I want to play? Why do I have to wear this when I want to wear that? The baby starts to look for its own tree of the knowledge of good and evil.

When the growing child declares its own independence and demands to make its own decisions, it claims authority for itself—and also receives responsibility for itself. It gets kicked out of its Garden of Eden.

All this is a natural process, good and healthy. It starts in early infancy and develops slowly until, at the end of adolescence, the child becomes an adult. The baby has taught the toddler, who has taught the child, who has taught the teenager, who teaches the adult. A poem I memorized in high school ends with the line, "The child is father of the man."

Many things happen in this long transition. An important one for this discussion is that the child discovers that parents are not God, only His stand-in. They discover that parents cannot solve all problems, do not know everything, and even make serious mistakes. Gods they are not.

Some children are afraid to give up the security of a perfect childhood. Things were easier when parents were responsible. Things were easier when someone else was in charge. As children they could thank their parents for providing for them. However, if they continue demanding that their parents take responsibility for all that happens, the appreciation turns to blame.

In his book *Where the Sidewalk Ends*, Shel Silverstein shares the poem, "I Won't Hatch." It tells of a chick in an egg who learns of the world of pollution, war, and other struggles. The chick says, "So I'm staying in here where it's safe and it's warm, and *I will not hatch*" (Harper and Row, © 1974, page 127). In the same way, the teenager or young adult may see a world of insurance payments, laundry, job, shopping lists, vacuum cleaners, and other symbols of adulthood and scream, "I will not hatch!"

Just as some members of Generation B refuse to give up control of their adult children, many children refuse to take responsibility for themselves, even though their birth records show they have reached the proper age. In nature, birds kick their offspring out of the nest and other animals abandon theirs at a certain age. Human parents seldom have it so easy.

> "After my divorce, I felt like I was a total failure. I had gone directly from my parents' home to my husband's home. It was his home—never ours. I couldn't handle the failure, so I went back to live with my parents. It felt so good to be under their roof again. It was security. It took me a long time to realize that it was also childhood."

This does not mean that adults who still claim that right of being children to their parents are always immature people. In many areas of their lives, they may be responsible, capable people. However, they may want their parents to be responsible in certain areas.

Here's an evaluation of someone in her own generation by a member of Generation C:

> *"When I first met Chuck, I thought, 'What a catch! How can he still be single?' He was 36 years old, nice looking, a successful professional person—and definitely not gay. Then I accidentally discovered that he took his lunch to work. His mother packed his lunch for him! Then I checked things out. He still lived at home. His mother cleaned his room, fixed his meals, and did much of his shopping. She even ironed his underwear! No way was I going to try to replace her."*

As children grow older, they do not plan to remain under their parents' authority any more than parents plan to continue to have authority over their children. From an objective point of view, both generations can recognize that they need their independence. But both sides often think there are certain exceptions in their case.

> *"I have some friends who have a 21-year-old son who still lives at home. They frequently complain about his immaturity and dependence on them. When I tried to tactfully suggest that maybe*

they should stop providing for him and make him become independent, they protested that he was not able to take care of himself. They insisted that, socially speaking, he was a 14-year-old and that they had to provide for him or he would not survive. One time I met their son, a fine, handsome young man with obvious abilities. I was shocked to discover that he agreed with his parents' evaluation. He had no desire to even think about leaving his parents' home and authority. Everything was fine as it was."

Other adult sons and daughters will continue to ask for their parents' authority and yet resent the parents for giving it.

"My daughter tells me she is divorcing her husband because he controls every detail of her life and that she wishes she could divorce me because I try to control her too. She wants to be far away from both her husband and me. Yet every time one of her children is sick, she asks me what to do. She wants me to tell her what to do if she gets a divorce. She wants me to tell her what job to take. It was easier to be her mother when she was a 3-year-old than it is now."

Just as Generation B must give up authority over their adult sons and daughters, so also adults must give up depending on the authority of their parents. The commandment about parents tells us to respect and honor our parents (Exodus 20:12). That commandment applies to people of all ages. A child shows respect to parents by obeying. Adult sons and daughters show respect in other ways.

If you are still trying to exercise control of your adult children's lives, you must change the situation. If parents complain that their adult offspring are still dependent, then they must move out of positions of authority. If the younger generation complains that parents are still trying to run their lives, the ones who complain must make the change.

Generation B, you need to realize that there have never been "perfect" parents. You may have made serious mistakes while raising your children, but now they are responsible for their lives. If they continue to live with resentment against you, the odds are that they will pass on more problems to their children than you did to them. As long as they blame you for their problems, they will live as children in their relationship to you. When they accept responsibility for themselves, they will act as adults. While you gave your adult children life because you conceived, delivered, and nourished them, they need to "get a life" to be in control of their own lives.

Is the Conflict over Money?

Money often becomes the arena for the battle over authority because whoever pays the bills makes the decisions. Money can be an important bargaining chip in the struggle between the generations. Money may be only an extension of the struggle for power, but because money can be added up to the last dollar and cent, and because one can charge interest on money, it must be treated as a separate part of the conflict between Generation B and Generation C.

All of us were born broke and without a stitch of clothes. St. Paul reminds us: "What did we bring into the world? Nothing! What can we take out of the world? Nothing!" (1 Timothy 6:7) By the way, the fact that we can take nothing with us through death is good news. A man over 90 taught me that lesson when he said, "If you think greed is bad now, think how bad it would be if we could take it with us." The point is that both the newborn and the dying need to depend on someone else. The infant depends on parents to provide. The dying depend on a Savior who has died and lives again.

But this book deals with the years between birth and death—specifically those years when it is difficult to be dependent on someone else and difficult to have someone depending on you. Who pays the bills? That is the question.

Who pays for what? when?

"As I watched my three sons grow up, I was amazed that they assumed everything in the house belonged to the family. The socks and underwear in my dresser drawer belonged to the family. They helped themselves at will. When they decided it was time to shave, they used my razor, which they saw as 'our' razor. Only as I watched my children

freely help themselves to things that I regarded as mine did I remember that I had done the same thing to my father."

In the beginning of the parent-child relationship, parents technically own everything, but what is theirs also belongs to their children, even in a legal sense. Over the years the children gradually obtain things that belong exclusively to them. They receive gifts, including money, that are theirs. They are given allowances, and they buy things that become theirs. Then comes the big day when children earn their first paycheck. As the children gradually collect their own assets, they do not automatically give up their claim on the family resources. From a teenage point of view, "What is mine is mine. What is my parents' is ours." The ideal situation is that over a period of 15 to 20 years, the children become adults and slowly increase their ability to provide for themselves at the same rate in which parental subsidy decreases.

But sometimes it doesn't work that way. Some children reach the age of adulthood and want the independence of adulthood but do not want to pay the price. In other cases the parents want to use money as a way to continue controlling their sons and daughters, even when they are no longer children.

"I remember the time our 22-year-old son invited his mother and me to dinner at an expensive restaurant. I had an urge to order a hamburger but suppressed it and went for the steak. I tried to think of ways

I could leave the tip or get the bill on my credit card. I knew I had to accept his hospitality. The odd part of this story is that as we walked back to his car, he found 20 bucks in the parking lot. I felt better—especially since I hadn't even thought of planting the lucky find there."

There is no age when children must become financially independent. The moment is recognized only after it happens. And even after it happens there may be financial dealings between the generations.

A member of Generation C says

"My parents promised to pay for my tuition and books through college. I wasn't ready for college after high school, even though I tried it. Now that I'm over 30, I see the need for that degree that used to be nothing but a piece of paper to me. But now my folks won't pay for my education. I don't think that's fair. What difference does it make? A buck is a buck."

Members of Generation B say

"We offered to send our son through college, but he didn't want to study. He asked for the money in cash rather than tuition and books, but we said no, that the offer was for education. Now that I am planning my retirement, he wants us to pay his tuition. We can't do it without messing up our retirement income."

"We learned from the mistakes made by some of our friends. When we talked to our children about college education, we put limits on the offer. We said we would pay for higher education up to the time they were 25—then they were on their own and so were we."

The question "Who pays for the wedding?" also ranks high as a cause for major misunderstandings between the generations. Over the years, weddings are discussed in the family. Parents and children react to the weddings of family and friends by making statements of approval or disapproval. Sometimes casual comments are heard as firm commitments, and firm commitments are heard as casual comments.

"When I was a teenager, my parents always made a big deal about weddings. Then they would talk about my wedding. It was a big deal to both of them. Dad could see himself walking me down the aisle. But I got married while I was in the military. We had a little wedding in the base chapel with no family present. It didn't last. Now I am getting married again and I would like the wedding my parents have always dreamed about. But they won't pay for it. They say that my fiancé and I are both employed, both mature, and we should take care of the wedding. It doesn't seem fair to me."

"We were very disappointed when our daughter got married without inviting us to the wed-

ding. We tried to make the best of it and had a party for our friends when she brought her husband home for a visit. Most of our friends gave them wedding gifts and none of them got a thank-you note. We don't feel right about inviting those friends to another wedding for the same daughter. We also don't feel right about paying for a wedding when we have no part in the planning. All she wants from us is the check."

Both tuition and weddings cause problems in many families because the expense comes at a time when Generation C has claimed independence by the very act of going away to school or by getting married. Generation B sees a light at the end of the tunnel after long years of using their time and money for children. They think they are now free to make plans for themselves. Meanwhile, Generation C sees the tuition or wedding as their parents' final payment on childhood.

Another part of the difficulty is that the plans, either formal or casual, were made by parents and children, but they are put into effect by parents and adult sons and daughters. When the plans were made, the parents were in charge. They made the decisions. They were part of the dreams. The teenagers accepted and even wanted their parents' involvement. That's the way things were in those days. But now the young adults see it as their education and their wedding; therefore, they make the decisions. Yet the decisions they make require financial support from their parents.

"When we were growing up, Dad told us that he would pay for our college educations if we chose the right career field. We all knew that he meant we would have to go to a church school for training as a professional church worker. That was fine when going to college just meant going to college. But after a number of 'career days' during the senior year of high school, I had a different view of college. But Dad wasn't there for the presentations. He already had made up his mind years before. I took a year out between high school and college to work as a waitress so I could pay my way to college."

Both generations experience frustration about the misunderstandings over tuition and weddings. In many cases, parents and children have had no problem on these subjects. Each generation feels that the solution is so simple.

- *Generation B:* "Why not do it the way we planned? We're paying the bills so we make decisions. That's the way it has always been."

- *Generation C:* "Why not do it the way we planned? It's our lives so we make the decisions. That's the way it's going to be from now on."

There is no simple solution to these struggles. If one generation wins and the other loses, there may be battle scars in the relationship for the rest of their lives. The solution that will prevent either side from winning or losing requires negotiation, compromise, and dependence on previous experiences of conflict resolution—but now as adults dealing with adults. No longer can Generation B use authority over their adult sons and daughters. Adult sons and daughters can no longer expect parents to pay for decisions that the younger generation makes.

The discussions about tuition and weddings may be difficult in some families. But the need to talk to one another also may be a great blessing for many families. The need to talk about who is responsible may be the push that establishes ways for the generations to live in cooperation and involvement in one another's lives. It is easy for families to develop a shallow method of communication about friends, clothes, and memories of the past. Such conversations are okay, but they don't require the attention to detail and to the other generation's point of view as plans for college and weddings do.

Not every family will have stress over the issue of who writes the check for tuition and the wedding reception. But even those who don't can understand the principle involved. Many big events happen during the years that it takes for Generation B to give up control of their adult sons and daughters and for Generation C to take responsibility for themselves. It is natural that weddings and college occur at that time. But there are other events that cause earth tremors as the two generations slide past each other. Consider the following and decide who pays the bill.

- The adult son or daughter has an opportunity to go to Europe (Mexico, Australia, or wherever) during summer break or right after graduation.

- Thanks for helping me get my undergraduate degree, Mom and Dad, but the counselor says it would be much better to go for my master's right away.
- I cannot live in the dorm one more week. They play handball in the hallway at 3 A.M. when I am studying. An apartment would only cost $_____ more per month.
- It's foolish for me to waste all this money on buses at school and planes when I come home for the holiday. It would be cheaper if I had a car.
- I have to buy a new computer. It's as necessary as a pencil box was for you when you were in the third grade.
- I've been asked to be in a friend's wedding. The dress (tux) and ticket will cost less than a thousand dollars. Isn't that a deal?

Each of the items (and the many more that you can add) are seen in two different ways.

Generation C sees those needs as their parents' last payment on their childhood. It's one more thing the parents can do for their offspring before the official financial break is made. After all, look at all the money you have invested for the last 21 (or even 31) years. This is such a small amount when compared to all the other things. If you help now, you will feel that you have finished your job.

Generation B sees all such items as an opportunity for their adult sons or daughters to really be adults. By paying for such things themselves, their sons and daughters are making a down payment on responsibility. Everyone has to learn how to make financial decisions. If parents pay the bill, their children have not learned to prioritize expenditures. If what they want is so important, they should give up something else to have it—just like parents have to when they foot the bill.

And the decision is_____!

Neither a borrower nor a lender be

One more financial pitfall. This starts as an innocent practice between parents and children. A 10-year-old daughter is invited to spend a weekend with her friend's family. She needs more money for her part of the entertainment, so she borrows an advance on her allowance. A son wants to buy a Mother's Day gift but doesn't have enough money. It's such a noble cause, so he goes to his father for help. Dad loans him five dollars.

These things happen all the time. In some cases the children pay the money back. In others, time goes by and the debt is forgotten.

This story also has a reverse plot. The parents are caught short on cash to pay the baby-sitter, so they borrow from the money the children got from Grandma. Or the parents stop at a convenience store to buy milk and bread, but they have no cash. They borrow a few bucks from the kids.

It happens all the time. In most cases the parents

pay the money back the next day—or the next week. Sometimes they forget, but the child doesn't.

Intra-family financing has many advantages: no long forms to fill out, no need for references, no papers to sign, and most of all, no interest to pay! It probably could be argued that it's good for parents to loan money to children and vice versa. Borrowing and loaning money is part of the real world.

But the real world also includes people who loan money to others as a way to keep control over them. It includes people who borrow money but don't repay it. It includes all kinds of opportunities for misunderstandings: "I thought it was a part of my Christmas gift from you." "I assumed you would pay interest." "I never thought you would buy a car while you still owe me money." "You never told me I had to pay it back by a certain date." And the list goes on.

A member of Generation C says

> *"My credit card company will trust me to use their money. I can borrow up to ten thousand dollars any time I want. But my parents won't loan me a dime. Makes you wonder, doesn't it?"*

A member of Generation B says

> *"The credit card company charges him more than 20 percent interest. We have loaned him money and never asked for any interest. The credit card company requires a minimum payment.*

When he has owed us money, he would refuse to even discuss a possible date for a payment."

Families are generally aware of what each person buys. They talk about the car, the stereo, the vacation, the new clothes. The one who has loaned the money always will feel a little resentment if the one who has borrowed the money buys some luxury item (in the opinion of the loaner). Normally it is not the parents' business how an adult son or daughter spends his or her own money. Nor is it Generation C's business how their parents spend money. But as soon as there is a debt involved, the normal rules are canceled. If you owe money to a bank, it will not know that you took four guests to an expensive restaurant. But members of your family will know.

Sometimes it is good from a financial point of view to loan money within the family. But make sure that it is also good for the relationships of family members. A few things must be discussed:

☐ Past credit records on family loans.

☐ Other debts and the priority of who gets paid first. (In a college loan to one of my sons, I discovered that the uncle—as in Sam—came before the father—as in me.)

☐ The income and job security of the borrower.

☐ Will there be interest? If so, how much and how will it be figured?

☐ Will the loan be paid off at one time or in installments?

☐ Will papers be signed?

In families with more than one child, parents also must consider the needs of the other children. It is not possible to treat each child alike when they are children nor can they be treated the same as adults. They have different needs, and those needs must be considered on individual terms. But all members need to be aware of any loan that amounts to "big bucks." Family secrets cause family fights. For large loans, a written agreement should be made about what happens in the event of the parents' death. Does the loan become the borrower's share of the estate? Will there be written records to show the amount of the debt? This concern is necessary not just for elderly or ill parents. Young and healthy people also die.

Then There's the Will

You've seen the bumper sticker "We are spending our children's inheritance." It is especially common on cars in Florida and Arizona but can be seen on cars with license plates from all over the country.

The will can be the way parents use finances to control their adult heirs up to, and even beyond, their death. "I'll cut you out of the will if ..." is a threat that puts the relationship on an auction block. On the other side, adult sons and daughters can express rejection of their parents by saying, "I don't want to inherit any of your money."

"My son rarely lets me see his daughter, so I was surprised when he and his wife arranged for

my granddaughter to spend a week with me. One day she said to me, 'My daddy said I had to be nice to you because you have lots of money.' "

Jesus tells a parable about a father and son. We call it the story of the prodigal son, though the word *prodigal* is not used in the Scriptures (Luke 15:11ff). *Prodigal* means wasteful or extravagant. Those who named the story thought that it was sad because the son wasted the father's wealth. But there is something much sadder than the waste of money. The son said, in effect, to his father, "I don't want to wait until you die to enjoy the use of your wealth. Let's pretend you are dead so I can inherit my share now." The father agreed to the son's plan. The joy of the story is that the son later realized that his father had a lot more to give him than money. Then he received forgiveness and love.

Nothing that I had worked for and earned meant a thing to me, because I knew that I would have to leave it to my successor, and he might be wise, or he might be foolish—who knows? Yet he will own everything I have worked for, everything my wisdom has earned for me in this world. It is all useless. So I came to regret that I had worked so hard. You work for something with all your wisdom, knowledge, and skill, and then you have to leave it all to someone who hasn't had to work for it. It is useless, and it isn't right! (Ecclesiastes 2:18–21)

Many people have deep regrets about their relationships with parents or children at the time of death—either their own death or the death of the other generation. Those who have had a difficult relationship with their parents often suffer more at the parents' death than those who have had a good relationship. Parents think that it is impossible for their children to die before they do, but it happens.

This book does not offer deathbed solutions. Rather, it encourages members of both generations to deal with all issues that cause problems in their relationship now. Don't let death—which will really divide you—be the cause for even more sorrow because you were already divided in this life. Let the life you can share now be the joy that helps you accept the failures of the other generations.

4

GREAT EXPECTATIONS

I once had a business lunch with two men who had recently moved to Arizona, one from California and the other from North Dakota. Both were in the market for a home. The one from California was elated because houses were so inexpensive. He was going to be able to buy a much larger home than his family had counted on. The man from North Dakota was depressed. Houses were much higher than he had expected. His family was going to have to downgrade their plans for a new home. Both families were looking at the same type of house, but they had different expectations.

Many families enjoy the relationship between generations B and C, not because the relationship is perfect but because it is better then they had expected. Other families experience stress and pain in the relationship between generations B and C, not because it is all bad but because it is not as good as they had expected. Family members need to understand not only their own expectations but also those of other members. You can't do any job well unless you know what is expected of you. Nor can you expect others to work to your satisfaction unless they know what you expect of them.

A Family Defines Itself

At one time the family was clearly defined by public image. Every family had a father and a mother. The father was about three inches taller and two years older than the mother. The number of children in that stereotypical family has gone down over the years, but there was always at least two—and always at least one of each gender. The father earned the income. The mother took care of the house. The children obeyed their parents, did well in school, and grew up to have their own families. A family lived in a house—not in an apartment, condo, or mobile home.

This is in no way a call to return to the "good old days." First, many families in the old days did not fit the description of the ideal family, but they kept quiet about it. In many situations, they felt like outcasts because they did not match community expectations. Second, the family that looked perfect outside the house may have been a disaster inside the house. The high community expectation of a family often caused many problems.

"My mother was always more concerned about appearances than feelings. She didn't seem to care how miserable we were as long as we appeared to be the happy family of her dreams. I hated it, but often I find myself putting the same unrealistic expectations on my children, even after they have grown up and left home."

Today, many families still fit that public image of a family from past generations. But many do not. Many families have one parent or one child. Many families include a mixture of generations. Often grandparents function as parents, and grandchildren are treated like sons and daughters. Families today include such a variety of stepchildren, stepparents, half-siblings, stepsiblings, etc., that it would be difficult to diagram all the possibilities for the nuclear family—let alone the extended family. According to the old system, each child got four grandparents. It's easy to imagine that some talk show will come up with a contest to see who can have the most grandparents, counting the parents and alternate parents of all the parents and alternate parents a child might have.

"I couldn't handle it when my father's new wife, who is five years older than I am, came up to my child at a family wedding and said, 'Give your grandmother a kiss.' I did not see that woman as my mother; therefore, I didn't see her as my child's grandmother. I had accepted her as my father's wife, but that was it."

This book will not update the definition of family according to current sociological trends nor will it call for a return to the old definition of family. Those tasks are for other people at other times. Before we can establish what the definition of a family should be, we have to understand how family members define family.

Please understand this point without belaboring the issue. It would be better if all families had one father and one mother, if all children lived with their biological parents and had a strong family base. It would be better, that is, if every adult and every child operated in the family because it is necessary for them to be a family. Many times that does not happen. Being in a family with one father, one mother, and the right number of children does not guarantee that all will be well with that family. Nor does it mean that the many people who live with the numerous variations of family structure are failures and that their children are doomed. The real issue is relationships—not statistics and diagrams of the perfect family.

> *"My wife and I each had a previous marriage, and we brought our children from those marriages into our own. We thought we did a pretty good job of raising our merged family. But when they grew up and had their own problems, including divorce and addictions, we blamed ourselves for all our kids' problems. One time in a Bible class we heard other parents talking about the problems they had with adult sons and daughters. Even though the parents in those families had no divorces on their record, their kids had the same problems as ours. We realized that we weren't helping anyone by blaming ourselves."*

Each individual needs to fine tune his or her definition of family and must understand that others in the family could have a different definition. Parents often will assume that their kids will see things as they do. Adult sons and daughters often will assume that their parents still see them as children. The following definitions are not an attempt to describe what a family should be. They are ways to help you understand your definitions and perhaps see the different definitions that other family members might have.

Attempts to identify parent and adult child roles have a double complication. There's not only the differences in generations but also in gender. Even our language shows subtle differences in attitudes. Notice, for example, we more often say "mother and father" rather than the reverse and "son and daughter" rather than the opposite. One time the female is named first more often, another time the male. We most often say "bride and groom" rather than "groom and bride." Later, though, it seems easier to say "husband and wife" instead of "wife and husband." Trying to become politically correct by revising the language doesn't solve the problem. Changing attitudes about ourselves and others will help.

Father

Let's skip the biological definition and get to the functional definition. To a small child, father provides protection, food, and direction. What is the role of a father to an adult son or daughter? Does he still have an authoritative role over them? Do they expect him to have that authority? Does he have an advisory role? Is he a figure of stability, a link in the chain to family roots? Does he want to give what his adult sons and daughters want to receive? Does he see his job as finished or redefined? Do his adult offspring see his job as finished or redefined? During the process of redefining the role of father, the two generations may come up with differing definitions.

"My dad never taught me how to fix things, like assembling something that you buy at Sears or to change a tire. I feel that he didn't give me what I need."

Father, as you look at your relationship with your adult sons and daughters, do you realize that they may see others in the same role? Do your adult children have stepfathers, fathers-in-law, grandfathers, or other father figures that share in some way in their lives? Do these other men replace you in your children's lives, or do they supplement your involvement as the father of an adult? Do you make it difficult for your children to be adults because you resent other father figures in their lives? Or did you bow out because you thought others had replaced you even though your adult offspring still need you to function as a father?

Mother

Is a mother just a female parent who fills the same function as a father once the birth process is complete? Or is there a special relationship between a mother and her adult sons and daughters that a father could not provide. In today's world, many mothers have shared equally with their husbands the responsibilities of earning the money to support their children, just as many fathers have shared in cooking and household chores. Is the only difference a matter of gender or a matter of function?

> *"We have four adult children all living out of state. My husband and I have noticed a strange thing about their phone calls. Rarely, do they call both of us. I'm not sure they are aware of it, but when they dial our phone number, they know which parent they want to talk to. Sometimes I answer and get a brief hello, then, 'Is Dad there?' Sometimes it's the other way around. But we know that they need each of us and that they have defined in their own minds what those needs are."*

Few adults are going to say, "I want my Mommy!" But all of us have felt that way. Some adult sons and daughters remember what they received from their mother (or father) as a child and still need the same support as an adult. Others also remember what they did not get from a mother and feel an emptiness.

> *"I think my mother always wanted to be my big sister rather than my mother. She never did the things that I think mothers ought to do. I don't remember that she ever baked cookies. She never taught me to sew. But she helped me learn how to*

use makeup and how to buy jewelry. A sister or an
aunt could do that."

Also, mothers, recognize that your adult sons and daughters may have other mother figures in their lives: stepmothers, mothers-in-law, aunts, grandmothers, etc. Perhaps you feel like a mother to a person who is not your son or daughter. That does not distract from your love and concern for your own sons and daughters. Understand that your children may have other mother figures, and do not let jealousy or rivalry become a part of your relationship with your adult children. Instead, look at the relationships that you have with adult sons and daughters. What do you have to offer that they need from you? Can you be glad for their sake that they can receive from someone else something that you cannot offer?

Son

What is your definition of your adult male offspring? Until recently, there was a clear understanding of the change when a son who is a child becomes an adult. At first he was "the son whom I take care of." Then he became "the son who takes care of me." Although the extreme definitions may still apply at the two ends of life, there are many years between the times when the parent-son relationship is described by who takes care of whom. Those in-between years are the subject of this book.

A boy soon learns that he will be compared to his parents, especially his father. He will be told that he looks like, walks like, or talks like his male parent. He will have his father's build, eyes, hair, etc. He is his father's son—in some cases his mother's son.

As the boy becomes a man, he feels a need for his own identity. He must be different than his father, if not in looks then in political and religious views, in values, in occupation. He sees the person he wants to become and looks to the future. Teenagers and young adults often see themselves as older than they are.

At a funeral, I noticed a conservatively dressed, middle-aged man who was wearing an earring. My curiosity made me get acquainted with that man because I had a feeling he would want to explain the out-of-place earring. He did. He said he had two adult sons who had their ears pierced and he didn't like it—so he did the same thing. As long as he wore an earring, they wouldn't. "It's the least I can do for them," he explained.

While teenagers and young adults see themselves as older than they are, parents see them as younger than they are. It sometimes shocks parents to realize that their adult sons and daughters are successful in business and other professional or community activities.

"When I was changing planes, I saw my son who was at the same airport to greet business associates who had flown in from Japan. I could not believe that young businessman was my son. He was conservatively dressed in a dark suit with a

button-down shirt. When we are together as a family, he wears wild shirts and shorts. He was confident and poised as he greeted people from another country. When he is with his brother and sisters, he acts like a kid."

Parents who put a bumper sticker on their car that says, "My child is an honor role student at Central Middle School," still find pride in their adult sons and daughters. The cliché of the parents who speak of "My son, the doctor" is very real. The parent still feels a sense of pride in the son or daughter. That pride may be expressed in a way that sounds like ownership.

Many sons must live up to high expectations set by parents. Sometimes they achieve far beyond their own goals but still feel like a failure because they perceive that they have not lived up to their parents' expectations. Just as parents may overrate their offspring's successes, they also may overstate their failures. Parents have been known to say, "My son, the dropout," or "My son, the welfare cheat." I once saw a bumper sticker that said, "My child is a trustee at San Quentin."

Daughter

The difference between a son and daughter is a matter of sexuality; therefore, it is a mystery. All parents know there is something special about having a daughter, just as there is something special about having a son. The difference can no longer be defined by their interest or lack of interest in sports, by their choices in vocations, by their achievements in school. To deny the difference between sons and daughters beyond physical traits that identify male and female is to deny reality. To explain that difference because of individual traits of one son or one daughter, as compared to others, doesn't help us understand why such traits are not consistent in all males or all females.

Many of the things said about a son in the previous section are also true about a daughter. But to ignore the differences would be to miss the blessing of God's intriguing idea to make us male and female.

A poem that I first heard when I got married, but also have heard at many wedding receptions since then, may seem out of step in today's world, but the idea is still part of many families.

> A daughter is a daughter all your life.
> A son is a son till he takes a wife.

As a parish pastor, I am a part of numerous weddings. And as the father of three sons, I don't quite get the question, "Who gives this woman to be married to this man?" My problem may simply be that I know the question will never be asked of me and that I think it also could be asked the other way around: "Who gives this man to be married to this woman?" I recognize that the fathers of daughters want "who gives ..." included. So be it.

However, I offer another set of questions in the wedding ceremony.

- *To the family of the bride:* "Will you accept (name) into your family?"

- *To the family of the groom:* "Will you accept (name) into your family?"

I have learned something about family attitudes toward sons and daughters by using these questions over many years. At most rehearsals, the bride's family will have fun with their question with remarks like "Maybe!" "Give us a chance to caucus on this one." "Can we put some limitations on that?"

However, in an equal number of cases, the groom's family will say things like "That's the best deal we've been offered today." "Yes, and we don't take returns." "We're getting the best of this deal."

Most families find it easier to marry off a son than a daughter.

Family

I know that I have been treading in dangerous waters as I asked you to think of your understanding of mother/father and son/daughter roles. All of us have both spiritually correct and politically correct definitions. But for this chapter, the issue is not what should be but what is. You need to know what you expect from your mother/father or your son/daughter. You also need to know what the other generation expects of you. As you grow in understanding of what you expect of others and what others expect of you, you may recognize that changes have to be made. But the changes in the behavior will not occur until the needed changes are made in expectations.

"For years I was miserable for the weeks before and after Mother's Day and my birthday. I thought that my sons should phone me. I expected cards and gifts. That's what I had done for my mother on her birthday and on Mother's Day. But my adult sons didn't do it. I dreaded both events until I realized that they were not going to change. I also realized that they did other things to show their love and appreciation for me—things I had not done for my mother. I had to learn to accept what they had to give, not what I wanted to receive."

Many families recycle pains year after year because they have different expectations of one another. Some even break the relationships because they cannot endure the repeated pain. The better solution is to understand and change the expectations.

Others Who Define Your Family

Many words have more than one meaning. The primary meaning has spinoffs that give different definitions. The primary definition of a family comes from the family itself. Each family has spelled out who mother, father, son, and daughter are. The definition changes as each person within the family changes.

However, there are many other influences that contribute to the definition of your family. Sometimes family members resent the outside influences that interfere in the way a family lives together. But the fact is that none of us can be the Swiss Family Robinson and live on an island by ourselves. We have to deal with the outside forces that shape the family.

The job

The same job that brings money into the family also brings control. The family schedule, address, vacation, and lifestyle all are greatly influenced by the jobs held by various members of the family. If both parents work outside the home, the difficulty in scheduling and in knowing where the family will live becomes even more difficult. When teenagers get jobs, there is even more conflict on the use of the family car, meals, and vacations. These problems carry into the adult relationships of parents and children.

> *"I hate my dad's job. His work kept him so busy or made him so tired that I always felt I came in second or third in his priorities. He kept telling me that he needed the job for the sake of the family. I didn't see it that way."*

Each member of the family knows the priorities of his or her own job and accepts them as necessary. Then each one expects the others in the family to respect the need for employment. Soon the family is controlled by outsiders—the bosses!

> *"Someone told me a story about a relative who was a doctor. The family planned a weekend trip and the doctor got someone to stand by to care for his patients. However, the family didn't get to go away—because the son couldn't find someone to*

take his paper route. I thought, 'How silly!' until
my kids got jobs. Now I understand."

Friends

"I wish our family was like ..." is often spoken by the younger generation and often thought by the older one. In our daily activities we see lots of other examples of families. Young adults can look at their friends' parents and wish that they could trade in their overbearing, uncaring, not involved, overly involved, or otherwise delinquent parents. Parents of young adults can see their friends' children and wish they could trade in their uncooperative, under-achieving, overassertive, manipulative, or otherwise unfinished adult sons and daughters.

"I work with a man about the age of one of my sons. My co-worker's father had been un-faithful to his mother and has been married three times. This young man seems to respect and appreciate his father more than my son does me. Yet my co-worker has even said to me that he wishes his father would have been like me. It's tempting to ask if we could go back to the hospitals where the younger generation was born and arrange a switch."

The thought of trading family members can be tempting, but it ignores the reality of the years a family has spent together. Other parents and their children may have been fortunate to have shared a good rela-

97

tionship during the years that the children were growing up. They may have worked hard to overcome problems and thereby have developed good methods of
communication in adult relationships. In other situations the relationship one sees between friends and their
parents (or adult sons and daughters) may not be as
perfect as it appears. Some families seem to get along
well because they have detached from one another.
Another family may have more struggles merely
because they have remained more closely bonded with
one another.

You will not help your own family relationships
by comparing your children to others. Each family is
its own unit and must live by its own needs. However, you will help yourself and others in your family if
you understand how you have been influenced by
others outside your family and how others in your
family also have outside influences.

If you have accepted the values, religious faith,
political attitudes, social needs, interests in recre-
ation, goals in life, etc., of your friends (who are mea-
surably different from your adult sons and daughters), those ideas will change your relationship with
your family. It does not mean that the relationship
must be destroyed, but it will become more limited.

If you are the one who has changed, you must
communicate your changes to your family. You cannot expect everyone in your family to make the
changes that you have made. You will need to help
other members of your family redefine their relationships to you according to who you are, not according

to who you were. Most of all, you cannot blame them because you have changed.

Next, if others in your family have made changes because they were influenced by those outside your family, you must recognize those changes. You cannot blame yourself because other adults in your family have chosen the lifestyle of friends or people you regard as outsiders. Your adult sons and daughters are responsible for themselves, and you are not the only influence in their lives. If you have changed, do not let your adult children blame it on midlife crisis, early senility, or other put-down assumptions. People will change as long as they live.

> *"My husband and I started going to church for the first time in our lives after our children left home. We sincerely wish we would have raised the kids in the church. We thought they would be happy for us. Instead, they acted like we joined some cult, and they blame our friends who invited us to church."*

To both generations: You may enjoy your friends more than your parents or your adult sons and daughters. You may turn to your friends for advice. You may share secrets with friends that you would never tell family members. But if you need heavy-duty help—if you need help that takes money, time, patience, and acceptance—it is your family that will provide that help.

In-laws

When a man and woman get married, they face many adjustments. One of the first is their definition of family. Biologically we need to marry someone outside our own family to bring in another set of genes. Our children are the products of two genetic trees. Sociologically, each marriage brings together two different definitions of family. The bride and groom each know what a family is from their own experiences—but their experiences are different. Each may have decided to reject something from his or her own family, but in the long run, each will bring much more that they accept from their childhood home.

This new family in Generation C must still relate to two families in Generation B. The Generation C family will have to merge some ideas about family, reject some, and develop some of their own concepts.

> *"I have two brothers and two sisters. As an adult I visit the home of one of my married sisters and feel at home because the menu and the way the food is served is like our childhood family. However, when I visit the home of one of my married brothers, I am a guest. The food is chosen and prepared as my sister-in-law learned from her home."*

Many newly married couples in Generation C feel heavy pressure from their parents as they try to define their own marriage and at the same time live with two sets of parents who know how a family should function. In some cases the young couple will accept one family and reject the other. In other cases, they reject the model of both sets of parents. Sometimes they opt to live with the pressure.

"My parents divorced when I was a kid so most of my childhood memories are pretty bad. But my wife came from a happy home. I feel closer to my father-in-law than I do to my own father. I want my kids to be raised like my wife was. I still love my parents and I especially respect my mother for what she did for me. But I see my in-laws as the example that I want to follow."

A better solution is to recognize the blessings from both families. Each childhood family has something to give to the new couple and to their children. For a newly married couple, the process of coping with the expectations of two families can be a good lesson in communication. First, they have to learn to talk to each other about the differences. They have to explain their own values and needs to each other. They also have to learn how to explain their decisions to their parents. All this is good practice in the skills of communication and, ideally, will help them be more understanding when their children grow up, get married, and become part of another family.

Meanwhile, as their sons and daughters marry, members of Generation B need to remember their own adjustment to the needs of two childhood families. If they try to hold on to their married sons and daughters, if they try to use guilt or other force to control their new in-laws, they may lose the relationship with their adult children—and future grandchildren.

Television and movies

Can you name a movie or a TV program that shows a family that seems real to you, one that you would use as an example for your own family? In the past, families were often shown as perfect parents with perfect children. It wasn't real. They were bad "good examples" because no one could be that way in real life. Now most of the examples show such dysfunctional relationships that they have become unreal on the opposite end of the scale. They serve as good "bad examples" because no one could want to live that way.

It's popular today to blame the media and the world of entertainment for the problems in the American family. One of the strong themes of this book is to get off the victim trip and quit blaming others. The argument over whether the media reflects reality or creates reality may be a worthwhile subject for academic debate, but the answer will not help you or your family. You are responsible for choosing what you watch and read, and you are responsible for digesting the same. If you use the image of family as portrayed on the stages and screens of our nation as an excuse for your own problems, you have helped endorse that bad public view. If on the other hand, you deal with the real issues in your own life and in the lives of your family members, you will be projecting your image to a community. You can live in a family that is not all good and not all bad but does have love, forgiveness, and acceptance.

You can make good use of movies and TV to help your family members understand one another. Watch for TV programs that deal with the issues between generations B and C. The relationship between those two generations is a frequent theme on "Frasier," "Mad about You," "Friends," and "Seinfeld." These programs may be reruns by the time you read this, but the same themes will be on their sitcom replacements. If members of both Generation B and Generation C watch these programs together (even if they live miles apart), they can discuss the foolishness and the wisdom of the TV characters. They will see that the characterizations of parents and adult sons and daughters are always overdone, but they may recognize a hint of themselves in the exaggerations. Talking about the TV characters may be a safe way to express feelings about your own family relationships.

VCRs also make it possible for you to suggest that your adult children watch a movie about the relationship between the two generations. By using a movie as an ice-breaker for conversation, you can state your opinion about how the people in the movie created or solved their problems. You can hear how others in your family react to the same situations.

What Does a Family Do?

As I collected material for this chapter, *Parade: The Sunday Newspaper Magazine* (December 11, 1994) carried its annual "The American Family Photography Contest." The winning pictures show families, from infants to great-grandparents, doing what families do. For the sake of this book, limit the idea to parents and their adult sons and daughters. Let your mind's eye be a camera and take pictures of what you see your family doing together.

Look over the following list and select the events you would photograph to show what you expect of your adult sons and daughters.

- ☐ Anniversaries
- ☐ Birthdays
- ☐ Christmas
- ☐ Eating out
- ☐ Leisure time
- ☐ Meals
- ☐ Shopping
- ☐ Sports events
- ☐ Sundays
- ☐ Vacations
- ☐ Worship

What would you add to the list? What would you eliminate from the list?

Now look at the list again from the point of view of your adult sons and daughters. What would they add to the list? What would they eliminate?

Notice that the first step just includes topics.

Items that may be very important to you may not even be on the list of the other generations in your family. Items that the other generations may consider high priorities may not be on your list at all. The first assignment is to understand and accept the differences in your list. Your adult offspring do not have to like everything you like. Equally true, you don't have to like everything they like. However, you must recognize the differences in expectations so you don't keep rediscovering the same conflicts. Some things you do together as a family, and some you don't.

> *"I dread birthdays and Christmas because my mother expects every one of us to be there. I love my family and I enjoy Mom's cooking, but I can't enjoy being together because it is forced. If I had a real invitation and choice about accepting it, I might even go. But we are drafted to be there."*

Next, think of the picture that you would take of the events that are on both your list and the list of others in your family. What picture would you take of your family celebrating Christmas, a birthday, going on vacation, eating together, etc.? Now think of how others in your family would take a picture of the same event. Do you agree on the subject but not the method of sharing the event?

> *"All my adult children and their children expect to come to my house for Christmas. I do the shopping and the cooking. Once in a while, one of them will bring a pie or a salad, but I cook the meal.*

They don't think about the work of cleaning house
before and after. Sure, I enjoy having them and I'd
be disappointed if I didn't see them at Christmas,
but I would enjoy seeing them just as much at their
house and at their dining-room table. I might even
take a pie along."

The purpose of this exercise is not for you to change your views or to give you a way to make others change their views. If you understand the differences in expectations, you do not have to face disappointments at times that are important to you. Nor do you have to live with guilt because you have failed someone else.

What You See Is What You Get

Most parents have great expectations for their children. They saw the beautiful baby who said such clever things. They are sure their child will become president (or at least one of the people who tells the president what to do). Often parents expect their children to live out their dreams. Many times they give up continuing education or other advancement opportunities to provide for their children. But the children become adults with their own dreams or lack of dreams. The parents may feel that all their work and sacrifices were wasted.

"I was visiting with a friend when her adult
son came walking across the church courtyard. He
had neither a beard nor a shave. His hair was a

mess. He wore one earring. His clothes neither fit nor matched. He was smoking. The mother said, 'Remember when he was little and cute?' "

There is a time when parents need to accept their adult children for what they are rather than what the parents expected them to be.

Young children see their parents as perfect. As they grow older they become disillusioned as they see their parents' faults.

"When my youngest son was 8, I heard him say, 'Ask my dad; he knows everything.' Eight years later I know he thought (though I never heard him say it), 'Don't ask my dad. He doesn't know anything.' Now he's almost 30 and I think he has a realistic view of me. He knows what I am and what I am not."

Just as parents must give up the dream of perfect adult children, children who mature have to give up the expectation that parents can fill all their needs. Honest expectations make honest relationships.

5

THEY COME BACK AND BRING MORE WITH THEM

I was depressed the first summer that all my children were away from home. I expressed my loneliness to an older friend. He replied, "Don't worry about it. They'll come back, and they'll bring more with them."

He was right. Even if your sons and daughters leave home as children (in your eyes), they will return as adults. Coming back in some cases means adults returning to live in their parents' home. But it also has a broader meaning in this book. There needs to be a time when a child-to-adult relationship between parents and children becomes an adult-to-adult alliance. There needs to be a sudden or gradual, real or symbolic, end of the parent-child connection and a recognition of the new adult relationship. Young adults need to recognize and define the new relationship. Parents and their adult sons and daughters need to figure out a way to live in the same house—at least once in a while, even if it is only for a few hours. They also must learn to live together on the same planet all the time.

They Bring Back a Spouse

The custom of dating is more than "practice time" for young males and females to get to know one another and to learn to establish adult relationships. It also is practice for both youth and parents to introduce another person into the family circle. Some of the most dramatic moments in a family's history occur when the parents are sitting at home waiting for a son or daughter to bring home a special friend. It's a long wait for both generations.

Members of Generation B say

"We always liked all our children's friends. They were always welcome in our home. But when Erick brought Glenda home, I was uncomfortable. I don't know why. She was attractive, intelligent, a Christian. I talked to my pastor about her, and he said that maybe I sensed that this was a serious relationship and that I didn't want to give Erick up to another woman. Maybe so. But it was difficult for me. It became a barrier between me and my son for a number of years because he married Glenda. It also put a barrier between me and my husband because he didn't agree with me. For me, this has been the most difficult thing in my family."

"We liked Nancy the first time Dan brought her home. Dan had never kept a girlfriend for more than a few months, so we were almost afraid to let ourselves like her too much. We were delighted that

the friendship continued and overjoyed when they came to show us the engagement ring."

Members of Generation C say

"Sometimes I think my parents like my wife more than they do me, but I'm glad about it. When they phone, they always spend more time visiting with her, and they like to plan special things to please her. I figured that it might be because I came from an all-boy family and they were glad to have a daughter. When I mentioned it to my wife, she asked me to think about how her father treats me so special. I hadn't noticed before, but she was right."

"It's taken me three years to rebuild a good relationship with my parents. They couldn't stand the girl I dated in college. They were totally unreasonable about it. It upset me that they wouldn't let me bring her home. I probably stayed with her longer because my parents were so bullheaded about it. When we did break up, it was not because of my parents' opinion. They had no valid reason to dislike her. But it still makes me uncomfortable when I take a girl home to meet my parents, even though they have not objected to any friend since that one."

The two extremes are part of the story line in many families. In most cases, the good may not be quite that good and in many, the bad may not be quite that bad. Still the tension is often there. The difficulty is not about a specific problem but a more general he/she's-just-not-the-right-person-for-our-daughter/son. At other times, one issue may define the problem.

"We adored our daughter-in-law from the first day we met her. We could see how happy she made our son. Because they were still in school when they married and then moved around for a while, we never visited in their home, but they came to see us often. All was well. After they had two children, our daughter-in-law gave up her job to stay home, and they bought a house. We went to see them— and couldn't believe it! It was a pigsty! Our son worked long hours and came home to a filthy house. He never seemed to mind and apparently made no attempt to clean up because we were coming. If he did, I would have hated to see it before. We have solved the problem for ourselves by staying in a hotel when we visit them. We still love our daughter-in-law but not in that house."

"When Elaine brought Stan home, we were pleased with him. He was different than our family, but we appreciated the difference. He was interesting. Only after they were married did we discover that he never held a job more than six months. It didn't seem to bother him to be out of work. When he did look for work, he just wanted to

make a little money for some special, and temporary, reason. I don't think he knows what the word career *means."*

In most cases parents and their sons- or daughters-in-law do not recognize the conflicts they have until the problems are well developed. Such problems also are compounded because the issues are not discussed between the parents and the in-laws. Instead, the parents express their dissatisfaction to their adult sons and daughters, and the in-laws express their conflict to their spouses. The adult sons or daughters become the bulletin board where their parents and their spouses post their complaints.

This is not good!

But what can be done? There are different answers for different generations.

Generation B: Parents, your vote in the decisions made by your adult sons and daughters has been cast already. When they are deciding whom they will marry and what kind of marriage they will have, you are out of the loop. Years before, you gave your input into their marriage as they saw what marriage means to you. You made some mistakes. That doesn't mean you are to blame for every mistake your children make, no matter how old they are. You did some things right, and they didn't learn. But you can't put your life and theirs on rewind and go back to relive lessons not learned. You can hope and pray they will figure it out later and remember what you taught them.

*"When my daughter told me that she was get-
ting married, I cried for three days. But she didn't
see my tears. I knew she was too young, not only
in years but also in maturity. The only possible
good thing I could see in my son-in-law-to-be was
that he was good-looking. I know that's not
enough. I knew I could not stop her marriage, so I
made the best of it. I became happy for her sake. I
know that I can't make her marriage work, but I
am going to do everything I can to help her—even
though I know that most often means that I have to
keep my opinion to myself."*

When God set up the ground rules for marriage,
He used a rib as an object lesson to show that they
were of one flesh, and He explained, "That is why a
man leaves his father and mother and is united with
his wife, and they become one" (Genesis 2:24). It is a
fair understanding of Scripture to reverse genders
and say, "That is why a woman leaves her father and
mother and is united with her husband, and they
become one."

See yourself as the mother and father who must
say good-bye to the son or daughter who gets married. You are giving up that relationship with the
child who has been the center of your life. If you try
to hold on to your former role as a parent, you will
either destroy your son or daughter's marriage or
you will lose your son or daughter.

Your adult sons and daughters and their spouses will define their marriage. You can be a part of that

marriage only if you accept their definition. If you demand control, you will cut yourself out. One word of caution: If they define their marriage by willingly asking for your influence and control, be very careful. Even though they still ask for help because it is a habit, they may resent the advice, cash, or control factors that you might give.

Now the message you must give to Generation C. You must tell your adult children that as parents, you cannot give them independence. I have heard of a groom who opened a wedding gift from his mother to find apron strings. It was a good symbol, and the mother must have been a wise woman. However, it was only a symbol that she was willing to give up control. It was his job to assume responsibility for his life.

Go back to the Emancipation Proclamation for the newly married in Genesis 2: "That is why a man leaves his father and mother and is united with his wife, and they become one." If you assume the responsibility to get married, you also assume the responsibility for that marriage. Marriage is not a lease with an option to buy; it is a commitment. As parents, you were not perfect, just as your children were not perfect. When they get married, they leave behind the problems of their parents. The good news is that they can take the good parts of what they learned about marriage.

When most young adults leave their parents' home, they have to sort through the things of their childhood. Some things they throw away. Some they leave at their parents' home. Some they take with them. Encourage your adult children to use the model of sorting things and sort through the emotions of their childhood. They can take the good experiences with them and throw the bad ones out. And be careful what they leave with you.

"I'm getting a divorce. I will be a single parent. I truly believe it is my parents' fault. They never prepared me for real life. I never heard them argue. My mother did what my father said, even though many times she had a better idea. She kept a perfect house. He made good money. We dressed in the right clothes. We went on the right vacations. I wasn't prepared for a marriage in the real world."

"My father physically and verbally abused my mother all the time. I never saw them hug or kiss. I never heard them talk about things—just argue. When I got married, I didn't have a clue about how to be a husband—let alone a father. Our marriage didn't have a chance because my parents never gave me a chance."

The people who told me the two stories do not know each other and I do not intend to introduce them. They wouldn't like each other because each would be a threat to the other's excuse. The woman in the first story thinks that life in the home of the second family would have helped her be more realistic about marriage. The man in the second story would feel that the first parents would have equipped him for marriage. In fact, neither were prepared for marriage, not because of their parents but because they were not ready "to leave father and mother." They took their excuses with them.

In words and actions, parents of young couples must say: "If you are already married and find conflicts in your marriage, you need to deal with those conflicts with your spouse. Neither we, as your parents, nor your in-laws are involved. You cannot solve the difficulty by letting us make your decisions. You have to make the changes in yourself and in your marriage."

> *"After I had been married for six months, I realized that my husband and I need to move far away from my family if our marriage is to survive. I can see how my parents, my aunts, and others still control me. I am not strong enough to stop it. But I love my husband and he tries to understand. I hope that together we can find the strength to move away."*

As a newly married man and woman define their relationship (which is a marriage-long experience), they do not have to write their parents out of their new family to fulfill the "leave father and mother" clause. Their parents may continue to be important parts of their lives. If they avoid contact with their parents, they will lose the joy of adult relationships with their parents. But it must be an adult-to-adult relationship based on future involvement. It cannot be based on past control. It can include all the love and caring of the past but the ways of expressing that love and caring change.

Next Come Grandchildren

The special relationship between grandparents and grandchildren, generations B and D in this book, is sometimes confusing and even frustrating for Generation C. Grandparents often have more money and time to give to their grandchildren than they did to their children. They are more relaxed. They don't have the full responsibility of parenting. They think their children will finally see what it was like to be mother and father and have a greater appreciation for them as parents.

The birth of grandchildren, in many cases, helps identify the relationship between generations B and C. The older generation sees their adult sons and daughters in a new light when they are also father and mother. The younger generation needs and appreciates the help their parents give with their new children—and they do realize for the first time the hard work and constant commitment required of parents. The addition of Generation D can provide a new start for generations B and C.

However, the introduction of another generation also can complicate the family's established way of living with one another. Generation C can be jealous of the attention given by grandparents to grandchildren. The grandparents may expect more (or less) involvement in the grandchildren's lives than the parents expect. The parents of the new grandchildren have two sets of grandparents to depend on (or to contend with). Trying to balance the expectations of each set of grandparents can cause enough pressure to make the young parents consider moving to another country.

> *"When our first baby was born, we lived near my parents. My mother wanted to take care of the baby all the time. The thought of paying her never crossed her mind or mine. Then we moved to be near my husband's family. My mother-in-law wanted to take care of our daughter—as a paid baby-sitter. She refused to keep her on Saturdays, expected me to pack a lunch, and charged more than any of my friends paid for the same service. I solved one problem by putting our daughter in a nursery. But I know I've caused some other problems."*

Young parents can use their children to control their parents. By words or actions they say, "If you don't provide free baby-sitting service, pay these bills, give these gifts (or many other items on a list of demands), I will move away, live in a place that is not safe for your grandchildren, go on welfare, and not let you see your grandchildren (or other items demanded for the release of hostages)."

> *"Our daughter asked us to help them with a down payment for a house. We didn't have the money to do it, and based on previous experience,*

we felt we should not loan our daughter and son-in-law money. So they moved into a filthy apartment in a dangerous neighborhood with two small children. We were worried all the time and were afraid to visit them. I finally helped them find a better apartment in a safe neighborhood for the same price. By then they had found out that they couldn't stand the bad place either, so we worked it out."

Grandchildren should not be bargaining chips in a struggle between generations B and C. Wise King Solomon proved who the real mother was in a judicial case by finding out which of the two women was willing to give up her rights for the sake of the child. His wisdom also may be used today. Grandparents may have to give up some of their dreams and joy regarding grandchildren rather than risk causing severe problems for those grandchildren. In some cases young parents may have to consider the needs of their children and their own ability as parents to make a decision about what's best for the children.

"My daughter was 17 when she had a baby—my first grandchild. She knew she was not mature enough to take care of the baby. At first I wanted to keep the baby. I had recently gone through a divorce, and with the help of a counselor, I admitted that I was not mature enough to take on a small baby again. Maybe the most mature thing that either my daughter or I have done was to admit we

couldn't give a child a good home. We both agreed
that the baby should be given up for adoption."

Sometimes parents will insist that their daughter
keep a child born out of wedlock because they can't
endure the thought of losing the grandchild. In some
cases they raise the child as their own—even to the
point of legally adopting the child. That may be a
good solution, but in some families, the struggle
between the young mother and her parents can cause
problems for all three generations.

"Our son fathered a child when he was 17.
Neither the girl nor her family were in any situa-
tion to raise the child, so we did. Our son is now
married and has a family. And we have a wonder-
ful little daughter who seems like a change-of-life
baby even though she is technically our grand-
child. She loves us as parents and her biological
father as a wonderful big brother. Things haven't
always been easy, but all of us have put our love for
the child first. That helped solve other problems."

Every family has its own special situations—
that's what weaves individuals into a family. The
more people involved, the more variations there are.
Grandchildren greatly increase the family census.
They are neither the cause of problems nor the solution. Grandchildren will give more ways to enjoy and
appreciate the good parts of the relationship between
generations B and C. They also will surface some
pains and difficulties that exist in that relationship.

The arrival of grandchildren can be seen as another opportunity to take an inventory of the family emotions. The results of the individual soul searching and sharing among family members may be a way to remove old problems and to gain an even greater appreciation of the good that exists.

When One Comes Home

It's the stuff sitcoms are made of. A middle-aged couple is enjoying the new freedom they have because all the children are out of the house. The husband and wife have time for each other. They have money. What more could they ask for? Then the phone or the doorbell rings and they discover that one of their adult sons or daughters wants to come back to live with them. It's funny on TV, but not in real life.

A problem always arises when an adult returns to live with parents. In some cases it could be a problem with the parents. Their health or financial situation may require an adult child to come back to help.

"I had great plans when I got out of the military, but at that time Dad lost his job and Mom had serious health problems. It was scary to realize that my parents were broke. So I lived with them so my rent payments could make their mortgage payment. I took a lot of guff from my friends about living with Mommy and Daddy, but I had to do it."

More often, the problem is brought home by an adult son or daughter and, in a few cases, an adult grandchild. The adult returns to the parental home because he or she has lost a job; been divorced; has a health problem; has a problem with alcohol, drugs, gambling, or other addiction; over-used the credit cards; or all the above, plus uncountable other things that I haven't heard about.

The adult moving home already has a problem, and part of the solution is (or at least seems to be) to move home. In some cases the move home will help. In others, it will add to the problem.

> *"I don't know how I would have made it without my parents after my divorce. At first I felt strange to be a 30-year-old guy living at home. But I got back my feeling of family. I learned again what it was like to talk and to listen. My parents were super."*

One obvious reason for a young adult to move back to the parents' home is that the rent is right. Few parents will charge their adult sons and daughters rent. If they do, it is often only a token amount and the parents often put the money in a special account so it still belongs to the adult child. Both generations often are uncomfortable about the financial arrangements when one moves in with the other. It is difficult, if not impossible, to establish a fair market price. In many cases the returning son or daughter could not pay a fair amount because finances are part of the problem.

> *"The one thing that bothers me about living with my dad is that I am not paying any of the*

household expenses. I buy groceries but do nothing about rent or utilities. I brought the subject up, but Dad was uncomfortable. I think he would feel bad about taking money from me, but I also get the feeling that he worries about letting me live in an unreal situation. We haven't worked this out. Maybe I'll move out before we do."

Generally, the issue of rent is not discussed in many families because the parents and the adult son or daughter think it is a visit rather than a change of residence. "Can I stay with you for just a short time?" is the usual request. Or "Why don't you live with us for a little while so you can get back on your feet?" is the offer. In either case, the deal was meant to be for weeks, but sometimes it extends into months and even years.

The obvious solution is for both generations to talk about the financial arrangements and to agree on a dollar amount and the length of stay—or at least a time when the figure would be renegotiated. Like most obvious solutions, this one is not easy. Parents are concerned about the other stresses in their offspring's life. Some families have never talked about money and this doesn't seem like a good time to start. Perhaps a third person—pastor, objective relative (if that is not a contradiction in terms), or a mutual friend—could help arrange a financial agreement.

Paying rent is one way for adult sons or daughters to maintain their adult status if they move back into their parents' home. But sometimes it is impossible. Many of the reasons adults must move back to their parents' home involve financial problems. Losing a job stops income. Divorce and sickness use up financial resources. Often parents recognize they cannot solve their adult children's problems, but they can help by offering a bedroom and refrigerator. In most cases it adds little to the parents' monthly expenses. It's the easiest way for parents to help.

Both generations need to ask some hard questions: Is this the best way for the parents to help? Would the adult son or daughter work out the problems in a marriage if he or she did not have parents to go home to? Would the members of Generation C accept a less desirable job if they did not have a comfortable home with Mom and Dad? Is the request for (or an offer of) free housing a way to let the adult sons or daughters get on their feet again? Or does it allow Generation B to keep control of their children's lives and Generation C to keep the title "adult children"?

These questions should not be seen as "either/or" situations. Rather, they are things to be discussed. If either generation refuses to talk about the reasons and terms of their living in the same home, problems will develop. Members of Generation B can feel good about giving help to their adult offspring—if it gives the son or daughter an opportunity to deal with the problem and get life going again. However, that same offer to help could allow Generation C to avoid dealing with the real problem. Members of Generation C can feel good about accepting help from their parents if it is a part of a plan for their recovery and future independence.

The question of paying rent is only the first, and perhaps the easiest, of the decisions that must be made. Who is responsible for the expenses and the shopping, cooking, cleaning, and laundry? How does each generation maintain privacy? Who controls the TV set? Who brings in the mail—and thereby spies on personal and business correspondence of the other generation?

> *"I was separated from my wife and trying to work things out in my marriage, so I moved in with my mother for a while. I got a personal letter from a female friend (handwritten return address). My mother put the letter on my bed. There was absolutely nothing wrong about receiving the letter. There was no possible romantic implication. My mother said nothing. But I had this compelling need to explain. I should have gotten a post office box."*

More questions: How does either generation invite guests without having to request permission? How does everyone handle drop-in company? Who answers the phone? How do you let others know you are expecting an important phone call so the phone won't be used for long conversations? Who is welcome to use the food in the pantry and the refrigerator?

> *"Our adult son was living with us temporarily. I had some special food in the cupboard that I was saving for a special event. I came home one day and found that my son had eaten the special*

treat as a snack. The fact that the food was expensive and hard to get was bad enough, but I felt he had violated my rights in helping himself to something without asking."

Notice that I am not giving the answers to all these questions because my answers would not fit your family. Nor do I think I have listed all the necessary questions. These are only thought starters. If you are going to have an adult son or daughter live with you, both you and the other generation must be willing to discuss the issues that could cause misunderstandings. It is much better to talk about such issues before they become problems. If one generation refuses to talk about the arrangements for sharing a home, that is a yellow (if not red) flag that says trouble lies ahead.

"I expected to be laid off from my job and had my résumé out. When it happened, I knew that I'd have another job in about three months but that I would have to move. So I accepted my parents' suggestion that I move back in with them until I knew where I would relocate. It sounded like a great idea, but it wasn't. Mom and Dad picked right back up from the time I left home. For the first week it was fun to be taken care of again. But before long I felt smothered. I didn't want to hurt my parents' feelings, and I needed a place to live. But frankly, the experience has not made me feel good about my parents."

"After my wife died, I asked our son to come live with me. He was single and I felt that he might need me as much as I needed him. After he moved in, he appointed himself my social director. He started telling me that I watched too much TV, that I needed more friends, that I needed to get more exercise. I was about ready to toss him out. Instead I told him I would manage my life and he could manage his. Now we get along fine."

The Problems Squared

If you are the parent of a single adult who has moved home, and if you share your story at a gathering of others your age, be prepared! Someone in the group is sure to top your story with one about the adult son or daughter who came home with a spouse. The problems are not just doubled. They are squared.

All the questions and concerns about the single returnee also apply to the adult married couple that moves back to live with one set of their parents. There are some extra problems.

In some cases the question may be asked: "Why come live with us? How about the other in-laws?" Perhaps there may be hurt feelings because your adult son or daughter and spouse chose to live with the spouse's parents rather than with you. Hurt feelings may be a cheap price to pay in the situation.

All the questions about privacy, decision making, and use of the facilities are complicated by the extra in-law. The returning son or daughter at least knows the routine of the home and already anticipates some of the possible difficulties. The in-law won't have a clue. In many cases the young adults are newly married and still working on their own adjustments to living with each other. Without a secure relationship of their own, they also will have to relate to others in the family.

The in-law also will have more of a guest image—both in his or her mind and in the minds of the parents-in-law. There may be even more discomfort about the privacy of bathrooms, personal laundry, mail, and phone calls. Add the complication of how the son- or daughter-in-law invites his or her own family to the home.

The addition of another person adds more stress on the use of TV and stereo. There is one more person to consider when one retires early and others roam around the house at night—then the reverse problem in the morning when the alarm clock wakes up everyone, though only one has to go to work.

Who works the daily crossword puzzle in the paper? Who cares for the pets and the plants? Who gets on whose nerves?

Again, my goal is not to ask every question but to assure each reader that difficulties will arise. Ask as many of the questions as possible when the arrangements are being made. Set an evaluation time at the end of the first month to see how the system is working and what can be done to improve it.

Of course, the potential problems increase if the young couple also has a child or children of their own. The grandparents' joy at having their grandchildren around full time may be replaced with the realization that their grandchildren are exactly like their own children were. Too many adults may complicate life for small children if each one, or each generation, has a different set of rules.

Practical Suggestions

1. *Ask each family member to write a review of this chapter. Each adult can list the ideas and questions that were helpful and suggest how they apply to your family. Each can find things that seem unrealistic, impossible, or possibly stupid—from the reviewer's point of view. Each one can add other needs.*

   When you compare your evaluations, you will have a good outline of your family's special needs and some suggestions for making the best of the situation.

2. *Watch for cartoons ("Cathy" in the daily comics will be a good place to start), jokes, and stories about generations B and C living in the same house or in the same community. Share your collections with the other adults and let everyone apply the message to your group. Some reactions: "That's exactly like us." "Thank God, we don't have that problem." "That's not funny because you do the same thing." "Why is it funny when they do it, but we get angry about the*

same thing?" "We don't have that problem because we ..."

3. *Pretend you are writing a sitcom for TV about a family in your situation. Identify all the people who live in your house and those who visit regularly (and therefore become part of the cast). Pick the actors to play the other family members—and the one to play yourself. Compare your choices with those of other family members.*

Write out some of the plots that would make programs for your family's TV sitcom. Can you see the humor in your situation? Can you see the pain and sorrow of other family members? Do other family members know how you feel about the events in your family life?

4. *Plan as many meals as possible for the entire household to sit at the same table and share their lives with one another.*

5. *Let everyone in the family add to this list.*

6. *Pray.*

6 Yours, Mine, Ours, and Theirs

Time for review: The relationship between parents and adult sons and daughters often (always?) includes complications and difficulties. These are compounded when adult sons and daughters get married and have children. More individuals become part of the cast of characters—each assuming he or she has the star role in the drama called "The Human Family."

The plot thickens when divorce and remarriage come onto the scene. This chapter continues to look at those adult sons and daughters who come home and bring more with them—whether it's to live or to attend normal family activities like holidays, birthdays, births, and funerals. In this chapter they bring not blood family members or first round in-laws, but extras acquired through divorce and remarriage or marriage to a widow or widower. The successes and failures of previous experiences with in-laws and grandchildren will be helpful if you also have to include ex-in-laws, stepchildren, stepchildren's other parents and grandparents, and an assorted list of other possibilities.

Your Experience with Divorce

In all social and moral issues, you can be more sure about right and wrong if neither you nor anyone near to you has personally faced the problem. Use the following list as a way to see how divorce and remarriage has personally affected you.

Who in your family has been divorced or has married a divorced person?

☐ You

☐ Your spouse

☐ Your parents

☐ Your children

☐ Your brothers or sisters

☐ Your grandparents

☐ Your mother- or father-in-law

☐ Your nieces or nephews

☐ Your grandchildren

Understand how much your life has been affected by all the possible divorces listed above. Your relationships with others in your family also have been affected by each of those divorces. Go through the list again and see how the lines of family connections become tangled, and often snarled, by divorce and remarriage.

Fifty years ago, most families could have gone far down the list, even to the bottom, without a single divorce. Now most families have numerous divorces. Years ago, a politician who had been divorced would have been severely criticized if he ran for the U.S.

presidency. Now it is hardly mentioned. Years ago, clergy did not get divorced. Later, those who did immediately resigned from the ministry. Now, many pastors have divorced and remarried.

The divorce epidemic is a major cause for concern for Christians. The problem cannot be solved by outlawing divorce. Those countries that have no legal way for divorce (Italy and Ireland until recently, Brazil still today) have even greater problems for women and children who are not protected by divorce laws. It is a problem that we must live with. Being against divorce and condemning those who have broken marriages will do nothing to help others, and it will hurt your relationship with them.

The problem at hand is not the national or social issue that you learn about through the media. This is the problem you know about from your own experience—the divorce that affects your family. The divorce may be legal, but it still hurts. Divorce becomes the death of a relationship, only there is no funeral to express grief for the past and to give hope for the future. Before you can deal with the difficulty that divorce and remarriage may cause in your family, you need to understand your own attitudes about divorce and know how you can or cannot cope with it.

The Christian View of Divorce

I write this book as a Christian, and I assume it will be read by Christians or at least by those who want to live by Christian values.

[Jesus said,] "It was also said, 'Anyone who divorces his wife must give her a written notice of divorce.' But now I tell you: if a man divorces his wife for any cause other than her unfaithfulness, then he is guilty of making her commit adultery if she marries again; and the man who marries her commits adultery also." (Matthew 5:31–32)

Some Pharisees came to [Jesus] and tried to trap Him by asking, "Does our Law allow a man to divorce his wife for whatever reason he wishes?"

Jesus answered, "Haven't you read the scripture that says that in the beginning the Creator made people male and female? And God said, 'For this reason a man will leave his father and mother and unite with his wife, and the two will become one.' So they are no longer two, but one. Man must not separate, then, what God has joined together."

The Pharisees asked Him, "Why, then, did Moses give the law for a man to hand his wife a divorce notice and send her away?"

Jesus answered, "Moses gave you permission to divorce your wives because you are so hard to teach. But it was not like that at the time of creation. I tell you, then, that any man who divorces his wife for any cause other than her unfaithfulness, commits adultery if he marries some other woman."

His disciples said to Him, "If this is how it is between a man and his wife, it is better not to marry."

Jesus answered, "This teaching does not apply to everyone, but only to those to whom God has given it. For there are different reasons why men cannot marry: some, because they are born that way; others, because men made them that way; and others do not marry for the sake of the Kingdom of heaven. Let him who can accept this teaching do so." (Matthew 19:3–12)

For me to state *the* Christian view on divorce would be presumptuous since many sincere Christians have different opinions. Jesus made that statement for us. Many Christians see His instructions on divorce and remarriage from different points of view. It will not be helpful for you to become part of that debate about whose view is right. Our concern now is not the spiritual, psychological, or legal issues of divorce. Instead we are concerned about the people who are affected by divorce. We want to see divorce not as a fault that must be condemned but as a problem that needs help.

In the past, most Christians regarded divorce as an unforgivable sin. Some still do. A divorced person, or at least one who remarried or who married a divorced person, was excommunicated from the church and often exiled from a family. Such action may seem to solve the problem for the church or

135

the family because it eliminates the person who has offended them. However, if the church and the family love the person who has broken his or her marriage vows, the exile only adds to another pain of separation.

While I cannot state a position on divorce for all Christians, I can make a statement about sin that all Christians accept:

> *If we say that we have no sin, we deceive ourselves, and there is no truth in us. But if we confess our sins to God, He will keep His promise and do what is right: He will forgive us our sins and purify us from all our wrongdoing. (1 John 1:8–9)*

> *God puts people right through their faith in Jesus Christ. God does this to all who believe in Christ, because there is no difference at all: everyone has sinned and is far away from God's saving presence. But by the free gift of God's grace all are put right with Him through Christ Jesus, who sets them free. (Romans 3:22–24)*

Divorce is sin. The defense for divorce is not, "I was right in getting the divorce." The defense is to plead guilty and to ask for forgiveness through Jesus Christ. Rarely, if ever, is a person totally innocent in divorce. It does no one any good to establish which partner in a failed marriage was less guilty. Innocence is not a human virtue. Often the guilt includes the things that happened (or didn't happen) in the marriage—as well as the way the two people entered the marriage at the beginning. Sin is part of the human condition and becomes part of each human experience—including marriage. Those who recognize their guilt and repent are forgiven because Jesus Christ has paid the penalty of our sin.

The Holy Spirit works through repentance and forgiveness to heal the people hurt in divorce. One woman told me:

> *"We hurt for many reasons when our son and wife divorced. Part of our problem was that we felt that they didn't deal with the problems in their marriage. They both just walked out. We were glad when he started to date a Christian girl and talked about getting married in the church. We hoped the priest would help our son deal with the issues of his first marriage. Instead, he had to fill out a lot of papers to prove that his first marriage wasn't real. They avoided dealing with the things that were wrong."*

It is easy for us to see how many Christians in the past didn't help people who were going through the pain of divorce. It was easier for the church, and for individual Christians, to avoid helping people by leading them to repentance and to faith in the Savior who forgives all sin. They solved the problem by getting rid of, or ignoring, the people involved in divorce.

On the other hand, some family members want others to divorce. They may not like the stepparent or the in-law and deliberately try to sabotage the relationship. They see a way of solving their problem by causing a divorce without thinking about the pain they may cause others.

>*"Hank and I talked about his three adult kids before we married. I was sure that he and I could handle any problems that might come between us because of them. But we made the mistake of talking to each other rather than to them. They did everything they could to prevent our marriage, then to destroy it. One of them told me about the ways Hank had hurt their mother. Another exaggerated stories about his other girlfriends between marriages. They embarrassed me in front of my family and friends. It was tough."*

>*"My parents never really liked Charlene. They put up with her, but when she and I started having problems, I made the mistake of telling my parents. Dad offered to pay for a divorce. In a way, he may have saved my marriage, though I am sure that was not his reason. I was forced to go back to work out the problems with my wife—and we did it."*

We need to recognize that we may fail to help people by ignoring the seriousness of divorce. Today, many people accept divorce as part of the routine of life. Many explain their divorces in such easy ways:

- "It just didn't work out."
- "Neither one of us was ready for marriage."

- "I have a right to be happy and that wasn't it."
- "We just couldn't get along with each other."
- "We got married too young."
- "We were too old and set in our ways."
- "I was on the rebound."

All these and other reasons show a lack of commitment to marriage. At one time, divorce was almost impossible to accept and many people suffered; today, divorce is too easily accepted and many people still suffer. Divorce is to be forgiven, not excused. Those who are divorced need to recognize their mistakes, both in establishing their marriage and in ending it. They need to receive the forgiveness that Christ gives them and to give that forgiveness to their ex-spouses.

> "A month before our son was to get married again, his ex-wife phoned him and wanted to deal with the problems of their previous marriage. Her intentions may have been great, but her timing was awful. We don't defend our son for the mistakes he made in his first marriage, but we were glad he worked on them with his pastor before he planned the second marriage. His ex-wife complicated things for him, and it didn't help her any."

When people divorce and remarry without dealing with the issues of a previous marriage, they bring the problems of the first relationship into the second.

The cycle of divorce, marriage, divorce, marriage can repeat. Each new marriage is built on the pain of a previously broken relationship. Some people avoid dealing with sin and repentance during and after a divorce by going to secular counselors during the divorce and to a justice of the peace for a second marriage. In other cases church leaders refuse to help people during the time of their divorce and their later remarriage; therefore, the divorced people are forced to seek help from outside the church.

Repentance, forgiveness, and healing through Christ offers another approach. It is married, divorced, single, married. That step of becoming single before even considering another relationship is of highest importance. The process of repentance and forgiveness helps a divorced person become single again. The guilt of the previous marriage is gone because Christ removes it. Both anger at and love for the previous spouse must end. Only then can a divorced person consider another relationship.

If You [Lord] kept a record of our sins, who could escape being condemned? But You forgive us, so that we should reverently obey You. (Psalm 130:3–4)

Love does not keep a record of wrongs. (1 Corinthians 13:5b)

God sent Jesus Christ to save us because we are sinners. His forgiveness means that He has removed the guilt and the memory of our sins. Application: God sent Jesus to help us through the pain of our divorce and the divorces of those whom we love. God does not hold our past guilt against us. We do not hold the past guilt of others against them.

Don't Add to the Pain of Divorce

I included this discussion of the theology of divorce and remarriage to help you in your relationship with your adult sons and daughters. Christians have a resource for forgiveness and renewal in the Gospel. However, sometimes they forget to ask the Spirit's help in using it.

Suggestions

- Divorce causes pain. Many divorces are necessary because the marriage causes even more pain. Even then, the pain of separation exists. God's law against divorce was given to protect us from suffering broken relationships. God never gives us a rule just to teach us discipline or to manipulate our lives. He wants what is best for us, yet He helps us when we choose second best. Remember the quote from Jesus: Divorce was wrong, but it was allowed by the law of Moses because people were hard to teach. So we are hard to teach today and we hurt because of divorce.

- If you get a divorce others will feel the pain also. If you are 50 years old and have adult children when you divorce, your sons and daughters will feel the pain. (Though I need to add that they also will feel the pain if you stay in a destructive marriage.) If you divorced when your children were young, the aftershocks of the divorce will continue forever.

"My biggest problem when I planned my wedding was the decision about which father should walk me down the aisle. My first father lived far away, and I only saw him several times a year. My second father was always there when I needed him. He was the one who acted like a father. I love both of them, and I have had problems with both of them. I walked down the aisle alone because I couldn't choose between them."

Parents who divorce have the responsibility to understand how their children—at any age— are affected. Do not pretend that the divorce does not hurt them and do not wallow in guilt about past problems. Instead, adjust your expectations of your relationship with your children to include the fact that they have to deal with your problems. Help them live with the complications your divorce and remarriage adds to their lives.

Also be aware how the divorce of your adult children affects you and others in your family. It is not just your son or daughter and his or her spouse who are getting the divorce. It will, in most cases, also break the relationship between you and your daughter- or son-in-law and between your child and his or her parents-in-law. This is part of the pain of divorce. Do not make your family join in the anger your adult child may express about his or her ex-spouse. Be clear about any relationship you might want to continue with your adult child's ex-spouse.

"We loved Mike because he was our daughter's husband. Then we loved him because he was the father of our grandchildren. After the divorce, we discovered that we love Mike because he is Mike. We aren't trying to get our daughter and him back together. That's their business. But Mike is welcome in our home. We are glad when he calls or writes."

• If you go through a divorce, be glad that others in your family feel the pain as well. They care about you. You need them and they need you. Let them help you. A divorce breaks the primary relationship in your life and that is bad enough. Do not let it destroy other relationships. If another person in your family gets a divorce, be aware that the person already has enough pain. Do not add to it. He or she needs your love and understanding, not your criticism.

When You Lose or Gain an In-law

The values that we claim and the things that we do are not always consistent. Some have said they could never tolerate a divorce in their family, but when it happened, they were supportive of the one who went through the divorce. Others have accepted divorce among their friends and distant relatives, but when it hits close to home, they can't handle it and reject the person who gets a divorce.

We have talked about divorce as a spiritual and a social concern. Now let's look at divorce as it has or might affect your family.

Check the feelings of Generation C. How much has your divorce disrupted your relationship with your adult sons and daughters? Do they have problems with one or both parents now because a divorce occurred a long time ago?

> *"I could hardly remember when my parents were together. When they divorced, my dad moved far away. He had no contact with us. For years my mother told me how bad he was, and she pointed to the fact that he never supported us, visited us, or gave us gifts. Only after I went through a divorce myself did I realize that the good-guy/bad-guy story makes no sense. My mother made herself too innocent and Dad too bad. So I found him. He had paid child support, but she didn't tell us. She had refused his phone calls and returned gifts that he sent. Now I feel as though I have lost both a father and a mother."*

If you divorced when your kids were adults, did you still fight over custody—if not in courts, then in the minds of the family? What could you have done to make your divorce less painful for your children? What can you do to make your divorce less painful for them?

"After they celebrated their 30th wedding anniversary, my parents got a divorce. I knew they had stayed together only until the last kid left home. They are both happier people now. I enjoy each of them more since they divorced. I think they should have faced reality and gotten the divorce long ago."

When members of Generation B get a divorce, the job of both generations is for members of Generation C to maintain a relationship with both parents. Parents need to encourage that by not forcing their adult children to take sides. Parents should never speak evil of the divorced spouse. Meanwhile, adult sons and daughters also have responsibilities. They should not take sides. Even if they feel one parent has hurt the other, they only will increase the problem if they make the offended parent a victim and aid and abet self-pity.

This cooperative attitude requires work from both generations. In some cases it is impossible. Then the responsibility falls on the most mature (not by age but by responsibility) to make the best of the situation, redefine relationships, and do damage control. Some husbands and wives divorce the children as well as the spouse. You cannot find an easy answer that fits every situation. But you can accept the reality of your situation and avoid adding to problems and making them permanent. Perhaps your parents used "time out" when your children were younger. You may have to take a "time out" after a divorce. Always include the possibility of future reconciliation between parents and adult sons and daughters.

Ways you can help Generation C

Understand that adult children are more important to parents than parents are to them. Illustration: It is more difficult for parents to face the death of an adult son or daughter than it is for adults to face the death of a parent. Any generation may expect to bury their parents, but no generation expects to bury their sons or daughters at any age.

Now apply this to divorce. Children of any age will be hurt if their parents get a divorce. But parents will, in most cases, have an even more difficult time if their adult sons or daughters are divorced.

Part of the extra pain in Generation B is that parents will feel they are partly responsible for the failed marriage of their children. They will remember their own marital difficulties. They will recall words and scenes that their young children heard and saw. They still may be dealing with problems regarding their own broken relationships. They may feel that they neglected to give their children enough time or failed to teach them values or faith. They may recall other failures in their relationship with their offspring as children. Even when offspring are adults, parents take responsibility for any faults in the generation that follows them.

Neither generation benefits from blaming the other for its own problems. When a person makes a decision to get married, he or she is accepting responsibility for the action. The act of "leaving father and mother" includes leaving behind blame. The maturity required for marriage includes the ability to be responsible for one's self.

Still, young people who have problems in their marriage often need the support of their parents. When a son or daughter recognizes a problem, it is natural to turn to parents for comfort and advice. However, be extremely careful when giving your adult children counsel regarding their marriage. Remember that they will see things from your point of view because they have established many of their opinions in your home. Your adult son's or daughter's opinions will be more like yours than his or her spouse's.

As parents, you cannot be impartial judges. In some cases, impartiality can have a reverse spin. Instead of defending an adult son or daughter in a marriage squabble, some parents will expect more of their offspring. They may be more critical of their son or daughter than their son- or daughter-in-law because they know more of their child's faults.

To you and your adult sons and daughters: If you go through a divorce, your primary pain will be in the relationship with the spouse and the adjustment to the loss of a marriage. Even though you are sure the divorce is necessary, or if you have no choice

147

in the matter, you will experience pain. You need one another's help. Your adult children also will suffer pain when you lose a spouse. In most cases, they will not know all the details, and perhaps it is best that they don't know. But understand that your adult child's view may be different than yours. Ask him or her to help you and other family members—and to help the ex-spouse.

Getting through a divorce is only the first step. You also need to establish new relationships with the parties of the divorce. If you divorce, you need to find new ways to relate to your adult children. Which parent will they visit for holidays and special family occasions? They will need to devote more time to two separated parents than two who read the same letter, share the same phone call, and live in the same home. They can't give a combo present to a mother and father who have different addresses. Yet they need both of you, and both of you need them.

Generation B, you have an even greater problem when your adult sons or daughters divorce. When parents divorce, you have divided equally related parents. If your children divorce, you lose an in-law. Or do you?

"We have one son, but we have two daughters-in-law. When Glen and his first wife, Sharon, got a divorce, we had a hard time. We finally told Sharon that we had not divorced her and did not feel that she had divorced us. She agreed. We still love her and see her often. We also love Glen's new wife and

accept her as a wonderful daughter-in-law. She had nothing to do with our son's first marriage. It takes a little tact at Christmas and other special times, but it can be done. We have found the most important thing is that we don't hide either relationship from the other daughter-in-law. Each one knows that we love the other."

But some families have the opposite experience.

"Our daughter-in-law, Amy, was the joy of our life. We were devastated when they told us they were getting a divorce, but the pain became even worse when Amy vented her anger on us. We had never interfered in their marriage—and she agrees with that. But her anger at our son now also includes anger at us. The pain is even more because she is trying to turn our grandchildren against us too. We have lost both a daughter-in-law and grandchildren."

When the Dust Has Settled

Please understand that each divorce is a private, personal event. Unlike weddings—that include parties, a big event at church, the family together, and announcements to friends—a divorce is done in private or in the presence of professional strangers. Very seldom is a representative of the church or the family present for the events of a divorce. Society has not established the proper way to announce a divorce.

(The only similarity between a wedding and a divorce is that both can be expensive.)

Each divorce causes emotional, spiritual, physical, and financial stress. It affects job performance. It includes the loss of friends and often a home. During the months before and after a divorce, those involved need the support of family. They need someone to listen when they want to talk and to leave them alone when they need personal time. If you are the one going through the divorce, let your family know how they can help you. If another member of your family is going through the divorce, ask them how you can, or can't, help.

After a divorce is over, the individuals and their families establish a new pattern of life. They must adapt to the financial settlement, the new home, children's visits, and eventually, new relationships. After the dust has settled, the divorced person and his or her family must face the reality of changed relationships and accept those changes. If they have lost some, they must accept that loss. If they have gained some, they must welcome the new members of the family.

Count the losses

Who were the casualties of the divorce in your family? Did you lose a mother, father, son, daughter, brother, sister, grandparent, grandchild, uncle, aunt, nephew, niece? Is the relationship a total loss or only downgraded?

"I have a grandson that I have not seen for 18 years and may never see again. Sometimes I look at a man his age in a crowd and wonder if it might be him. I ask, 'Could we have been at the same airport at the same time? Could we have passed each other on a road?' "

"The first time our family was together after one daughter's divorce, a sad thing happened. Our 3-year-old grandson went around the house asking, 'Where is Uncle Ed?' No one had told him about the divorce."

"When I was little, I spent a lot of time with my grandparents. My best childhood memories are with them. After my parents divorced, my mother and I moved to another state. I still saw my grandparents one weekend a year, but it was never the same. I was a guest instead of a member of the family."

Part of the aftershocks of a divorce is to accept the losses and the restrictions on relationships. Mourn the losses and make the most of limited relationships, but do not live in the past. Make the best of limited relationships and look to the future. Perhaps the restrictions can be removed by accepting the less-than-desirable conditions now. By showing love and acceptance now, the future may be better. Your emotional stability and acceptance is best for you and will be the best help for others.

There will be a time when you need to update your house according to the losses. Which family pictures must be put away? Which ones will be thrown away? Are some gifts from an ex-in-law a bad reminder to you? Do you need to put the gift away or give it away? Do you need to keep certain cards, letters, or other items just as you would keep them if the person had died? There will be other questions that you must ask—and answer—for yourself. Accept the fact that others in the family may have different answers.

> *"I had been divorced for more than three years when I took my new fiancé home to meet my parents. When we came into my parents' living room and saw the last family picture still on the wall, I became upset. I knew it included my ex-husband. Then I noticed something different. The ex-husband had been standing at the end of a line of family members. My mother had cut him off the picture. My fiancé never noticed the missing family member."*

Count the gains

Strange as it may sound, the body count after the war of divorce may give you new relationships that are rewarding to you and others.

> *"When our daughter got married, she and her husband established a private life. From our point of view, they had a good relationship with each other but they had a limited relationship with our*

family and with his. They were with us for impor-
tant events but we were not as close as we would
have liked. We were surprised and sad when they
got a divorce. Then a strange thing happened—we
got our daughter back. She was again involved
with us like she had been before her marriage. She
has remarried again, but she is as close to us as she
was before her first marriage. And our new son-in-
law seems much more like a son than her first hus-
band did."

"We accepted our son's divorce because we had
no other choice and because, frankly, we knew they
did not have a good marriage. They were not able
to have children, which we understood, knowing
that it was not their decision. Then he remarried a
woman who had two sons and a daughter. When he
first told us about the children, we were not com-
fortable with the idea. But when we met them, they
were our grandchildren! We couldn't believe how
easy it was for them and for us to become a family.
Do you want to see their pictures?"

New members of the family gained through
divorce (or death of a spouse) and remarriage can be
a joy or a sorrow, but it is always complicated. Each
additional person brings another character into the
family drama. Each has special needs, special problems, and his or her own sense of timing. One will
want to accept and be accepted immediately. Anoth-

er will want to test out the new relationships before making commitments. Each will think that his or her way is the right way.

> *"When our three sons were small, we tried to adopt a daughter. One of the agency requirements was a letter from both my parents and my wife's parents giving their approval of the adoption. At first I resented the idea of asking my parents' approval when I was 34 years old. But the social worker explained that they wanted to know the grandparents would treat the adopted children the same as the other grandchildren. She wanted to know that they would be treated the same on birthdays, Christmas, vacations, and even in the grandparents' wills. Now I think it was a good idea."*

> *"I dread going to a family gathering at my husband's home because I know that our children (they call them "her" children) will be treated differently. One time, there were too many guests for the dining-room tables so our children were selected to eat in the kitchen. They got pats on the back rather than hugs."*

Divorce and remarriage creates new relationships that do not fit on the simple drawing of the family tree. The typical remarried family may have children that are "yours, mine, and ours." But not all divorce/remarriage situations are typical. It is possible to have a family that includes "yours, mine, ours, and theirs." For example: Your son's new wife has two children who become your stepgrandchildren. Those stepgrandchildren have two half-sisters that spend vacation and holidays with your son's new family. Your stepgrandchildren's half-siblings are not related to you, but they are present when you open your Christmas gifts. Get the problem?

> *"Two days before Christmas I received a call from my wife's niece, who happens to live in the same small town as my stepdaughter's biological father (my wife's ex-husband). He had not contacted my stepdaughter since she was 3 years old—15 years ago. Now my wife's niece said that this man's sister told her that he wanted to phone my stepdaughter for Christmas but wanted my permission. Suddenly, our Christmas plans were being upset by people we didn't even know! My wife and I did not want to refuse our daughter the right to talk to her biological father. We decided to call the ex-husband's sister since she was the contact person. We discovered that the idea of the phone call came from her, not my wife's ex-husband. It was her idea to create a relationship that never existed. Her good intentions made a mess for everyone."*

Each divorce and remarriage doubles the number of people who become involved in the family, even though many are not legally or socially a part of your family. The descriptions of possible "theirs" relationships would take more space than is available and the effort would not be helpful. The point is that family members must be treated according to their needs, not according to their legal standing.

You can choose how to relate to those who are really not related to you. You can try to exclude them from your family so you can devote more love and attention to those who are yours by blood or by first marriages or wherever else you draw your line. It will keep alive the issues of old relationships and old problems.

Your other choice is to accept those that other members of your family have brought into your family. Follow this line of thought: Because you love your son, you love his wife. Because you love your daughter-in-law, you love her two children by a previous marriage. Because you love your stepgrandchildren, you love their half-sisters. Continue this line of thinking as long as necessary. It helps to remember that Jesus is central even in this unusual family tree: Remind yourself that because Jesus loves you, you love Him, and therefore you can love (now go through the list again).

Through remarriages people gain grandchildren, grandparents, uncles, aunts, and cousins that they would not have otherwise had. Your life may be richer in both the love you receive and the love you give despite the pain and sorrow of divorce and remarriage. This does not mean divorce has become a good thing; it means God loves and helps people even when they do wrong.

Joseph said to [his brothers who had sold him as a slave], "Don't be afraid; I can't put myself in the place of God. You plotted evil against me, but God turned it into good, in order to preserve the lives of many people who are alive today because of what happened." (Genesis 50:19–20)

7
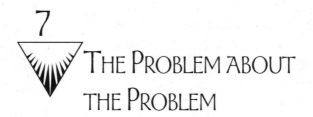
THE PROBLEM ABOUT
THE PROBLEM

All people have problems. Since it's something we all have in common, one might think it would be a bond among us. We could organize picnics for people with problems. We could have a parade on Problem Day and no one would go to watch it because we'd all be in the parade!

But it doesn't work that way. Problems do not always unite us—they often divide us. Our problems make us think about ourselves and forget others. Our problems often seem like big secrets that no one else must know. Our problems make us suspicious of others and afraid to ask for help. Our problems make us look for faults in others so we can find someone else who is worse off—and make ourselves feel better by comparison. Problems are a pain.

When parents have problems, the difficulties affect their children, even if they are adults. Parents also are affected by their children's problems, even when the children are adults and live on their own. Problems are an important part of the relationships between parents and their adult sons and daughters.

In many cases, people better solve, or at least live with, their problems because they share them with their family. In other cases, each problem adds more stress to the relationship of parents and their adult sons and daughters. Not only do they have problems, but they also have problems about the problems. Those "second-degree" problems or "problems-in-law" often are caused by family members. And each of us cause such problems for others in our families.

Divorce is one of those problems. Because it is so common and because it affects all extended families, it was treated in a separate chapter.

Now let's list other problems that may affect one person directly and also involve all other family members. Please read through the following list, carefully naming each problem. Many do not affect you or your family. Others are things that you think about, and worry about, every day. Still others are vague possibilities and you wonder if they could be a part of the plot of your family's story. Still others are denied, but they are there.

Family Problem List

☐ Abortion	☐ Bankruptcy
☐ Adoption	☐ Cancer
☐ AIDS	☐ Chronic illness
☐ Alcoholism	☐ Debt
☐ Anger	☐ Depression
☐ Anorexia	☐ Drug addiction

☐ Fire	☐ Physical disability
☐ Gambling	☐ Prejudice
☐ Homosexuality	☐ Pride
☐ Imprisonment	☐ Pyromania
☐ Inadequate housing	☐ Religious divisions
☐ Incest	☐ Revenge
☐ Job loss	☐ Sexual abuse
☐ Kleptomania	☐ Sexual dysfunction
☐ Loneliness	☐ Sleepiness
☐ Low self-esteem	☐ Smoking
☐ Mental illness	☐ Superstition
☐ Natural disasters	☐ Verbal abuse
☐ Obesity	☐ Violence
☐ Physical abuse	☐ Workaholism

Each problem listed (and others that you would add) affects many individuals and, therefore, also affects families. This chapter will not deal with each problem, but it will help families help one another deal with problems rather than create new problems.

What Is the Problem?

First, go through the list and check each item you think is your personal problem. Add other problems that are not on the list. If an item is confidential, put a code word like "The Big One" for the first, "The Big Second" for the next, etc. Name the problem to yourself even if you are not comfortable listing it.

After you have finished identifying your problems, ask yourself: "Do my adult sons and daughters know that I have these problems?" Here's a few questions to keep you thinking: Would others in your family be surprised to know the problems on your list? Do they not know about your need because you have hidden your problem or because they have not been sensitive to your feelings? Do you and others in your family avoid talking about certain issues so they are unaware of the issues that worry you?

> "From the time I was 8 until about 14, my uncle used every opportunity he had (and those that he could especially create) to touch my body or to talk about sex to me. He never molested me in a legal sense of the word, but I felt violated all the time. And I couldn't tell anyone. He was the favorite uncle and in-law for the rest of the family. My mother will never understand why I found an excuse to avoid his funeral. I have talked to a counselor about this problem, but I no longer think it necessary to tell my parents."

Now for the next step. Imagine that each of your adult sons and daughters went through the problem list with you in mind. What would they check as your problem? What would they add to the list? Do they think that you deny your real problems? Do you know the issues about you that worry them?

> "My relationship with my son became so bad that I asked him to go to a counselor with me. I

was surprised that he did. We each saw the same counselor separately. Afterwards, the counselor told us that our relationship had deteriorated so badly that we did not even have the same problems about each other. I did not know what troubled him about me, and he did not know what troubled me about him. The counselor told us that if we were to live as father and son we had to spend time listening to each other before we could talk to each other."

Now reverse the process. Go through the problem list thinking about each of your adult sons and daughters. Put an X and their initial by each item that—from your point of view—is a problem for one of your family members. Add any subjects that you see as their problems. Would they be surprised to know that you think they have these problems? Is it possible that they have problems about which you don't have a clue?

Among counselors, there is a rule of thumb that says, "The more healthy person in any relationship must be the first one to look for help." If you have difficult family relationships and are reading this book, it shows you are healthy enough to look for help. In doing the exercise above, you may realize that others do not want to deal with the issues that concern you. You cannot force them, but you can get help beyond this book. Part of your healing will be your effort to reach out to others in the family.

"Years ago I wrote to my father and told him how painful much of our relationship was to me—and how sorry I was for my contribution to the whole mess. I asked him to forgive me, and I told him I was willing to forgive him and start again. One year later, and I mean one year later, my parents called and acted as though nothing had transpired. I asked them if they had received my letter. My dad asked, 'What letter?' I repeated my question several times before my mother said, 'Yes, we did receive your letter.' My dad justified himself by saying that he did not consider the things in my letter important."

The goal of the exercise suggested above is to identify the problems that your family must deal with. Perhaps you are causing problems about the problems because you do not know what they are. If you each have a different answer to the question "What is the problem?" you cannot work together or help one another reach a solution. Agreeing on the identity of the problem is the first step in looking for an answer.

One more point about problems: They never come as singles. We all have a variety of problems that overlap in our own lives, and they also are intertwined with others around us. The stories that are in this book (as in all anecdotal material) seem to imply that each situation is the only problem the family has. Wrong! These are the problems discussed here because they are the ones that affect family relationships.

Is It a Problem?

The first big hurdle is to recognize that all family members will never even agree on the definition of a problem. You may feel that another member of the family has a serious problem, such as racial prejudice, homosexuality, alcohol dependency, or excessive anger, but the other person may not think it is a problem. If you try to discuss it, the other person may say, "I don't have a problem with it, so why should you?" The other person's attitude may be, "I've accepted myself as I am. If you love me, you will do the same."

Some people might be offended at some of the items on the problem list. For example, many people see adoption as a blessing, not a problem. However, others have given a child up for adoption, are adopted, or regret having adopted a child. This step requires that you admit your own problems and accept the fact that others in your family name other subjects as problems—even if you think they are not. Many people will start talking about a subject by saying, "I know I shouldn't feel this way, but ..." If you, or others, do feel that way, you must be willing to deal with the feelings rather than pass judgment on them. If your feelings do need to change, you must be willing to recognize them and find the way to change. The same goes for other members of your family.

Think about some of the reasons one may think a certain situation is a problem and another sees no problem.

A difference in moral principles

People have two basic ways of establishing moral principles. One is to make decisions on the basis of law and order, namely the political and social systems. The other way is by our relationship with God. As you might guess, the choices have a significant effect on how we function in families.

When moral principles are based on the political and social system, we have laws—and the violations are called crimes. The laws of our society change frequently. At one time, it was a crime in many states to swear in the presence of a lady. In some areas, it is a violation of social custom (and sometimes also the law) to work on Sunday. Some of the biggest legal issues today are about homosexuality, abortion, euthanasia, and the use of certain drugs. Are these things crimes? If they are not, some people will say they ought to be. If they are, some people will say they shouldn't be. Different people and different societies will give different answers.

Rather than evaluate each moral situation, this book will help family members understand the reasons why they don't understand one another. If you were to mark items on the problem list that you think are crimes, would you choose the same items as others in your family? If you have different assumptions, you always will have disagreements in your discussions. You will have problems about your problems.

Though crimes may be committed by individuals or gangs, members of the criminal's family are involved. They will share in the emotional, social, and financial burdens that result from crimes committed by a family member. In some cases, they even abet a criminal by not reporting his or her illegal actions. Family members have to decide how they will respond to the criminal actions of others.

"By the time our son was 18 years old, he was involved in drugs, often stayed out all night and slept all day, started or finished many a brawl, and was shot at least once that we know. He also was breaking into houses and stealing. Nothing we said seemed to make any impression on him, except to make matters worse. In desperation, we issued an ultimatum: You have one month to find yourself a job and an apartment. When the month was almost over, he asked, 'What can I do to stay?' We said, 'Nothing. You have to leave so when you come by to visit we'll be glad to see you and want to invite you in. And that can't happen if we're always at each other's throats the way we are now.' That was a long time ago. It took awhile, but he does come by. It makes no difference if he's alone or with his wife and children, we're genuinely glad to see him. God has indeed brought joy through the mourning!"

Suppose a man has a son who is stubborn and rebellious, a son who will not obey his parents, even though they punish him. His parents are to take him before the leaders of the town where he lives and make him stand trial. They are to say to

*them, "Our son is stubborn and rebellious and
refuses to obey us; he wastes money and is a drunk-
ard." (Deuteronomy 21:18–20)*

If we're to follow the prescription in Deuteronomy for dealing with this rebellious son, the punishment would be death by stoning to prevent future
disobedience on the part of others. It seems like a
fearsome way to introduce the other way we humans
establish moral principles. These are principles based
on our relationship with God. But before you shut
this system off, read on—carefully and thoughtfully.

God is our creator; therefore, He wrote the
User's Manual. He is in charge, so He tells us what is
right and what is wrong. When we talk about our
relationship with God, we use the word *sin* rather
than *crime*. Sin is a spiritual word, and without God,
there is no concept of sin.

Not everyone who uses the same User's Manual
will agree on the definition of sin. All Christians recognize that they are sinners in a generic sense, but
they disagree on the brand names. Some think it is a
sin to drink any alcohol, some think it is a sin to get
drunk, and some think the use of alcohol is optional.
When does the use of alcohol become a sin? When
does it become a crime? Different answers come from
different people.

Back to the problem list. How many of the items
on the list would you think of as a sin or as something
caused by sin? Is all obesity the result of the sin of
gluttony or is some caused by a physical disorder? If

you save too much money, are you guilty of greed? If you spend too much, are you guilty of irresponsibility toward yourself and others?

By asking such questions, I am not looking for a gray area between right and wrong. Rather, I am asking you to recognize that you are not the one who draws the line between what is right and what is wrong. God has done that, and all of us are below the line of holiness that He demands. Jesus Christ brought His holiness from above the line when He came to live with us below the line. By His death our sins are forgiven. We can deal with our own problem of sin—and can help others with their problem of sin—not when we condemn ourselves or others, but when we see our sin as evidence that we all need Christ.

The problem in the family is not that some draw the line between good and evil at different places. The problem is that all are sinners. Family members help one another by sharing the Savior who forgives all sin. They hurt one another if they take the responsibility of judging and punishing others for their sin.

"I love my daughter and I know she is a lesbian. I believe it is wrong for her to have a sexual relationship with another woman. Yet I love her, even as I know Jesus loves me even though I am a sinner. The difference is that I repent of my sin. I think she defends hers, though she says she believes in Jesus and knows she needs His forgiveness. I hurt because of this problem, but I know one thing.

I will help her more if I love her than if I condemn her. I learned that from Jesus."

Sin is a problem. It is a problem between us and God and between us and our loved ones. We create a problem about the problem of sin when we try to deal with it ourselves. Our own sin affects the way we see sin in ourselves and others. Therefore, we cannot depend on ourselves, or other sinners, to be right about sin.

[Jesus said,] "When [the Holy Spirit] comes, He will prove to the people of the world that they are wrong about sin and about what is right and about God's judgment." (John 16:8)

Now for the application. If you believe that a member of your family is doing something that is sinful but does not see it is wrong, do not let this destroy your relationship. You do not need to change your view of sin to still love that person. God knows more about our sin than anyone else—even *more* than we know about ourselves. But God still loves us and does something to help us with our problem of sin.

God would not have done us a favor if He had ignored or approved of our sins. Had He done either, we still would have the problems that our sins cause—and God would have left us on our own. Instead, He sent Jesus Christ to die for our sins. We never help a person by approving of something that is sinful. Paul wrote, "[Those who sin] know that God's law says that people who live in this way deserve death. Yet, not only do they continue to do these very things, but they even approve of others who do them" (Romans 1:32).

This is the place where you put into practice the simple guideline, "Hate the sin, but love the sinner." It is easier said than done. In reality many people ignore the sin and hate the sinner. One way to help the sinner is to remember that the member of your family has sins other than the one that offends you. Show that you believe the other sins are forgiven. Make use of the Christian privilege of repentance for yourself and show that you believe you are forgiven—not because you defend your sin but because God has forgiven it in Christ. Some people are afraid to admit certain sins because they know that repentance requires a desire to change and they are afraid they can't change. They are afraid to take the risk of asking for help from you or from Jesus. Your best solution is to apply the Gospel to yourself and your continuing struggle with guilt. Share that experience with the member of your family who also needs it. Do not say, by word or by attitude, "I know I am a sinner too, but thank God that my sins are not as bad as yours."

Next, if you believe that a family member has a problem with sin but sees no problem, do not decide you must punish the person. If you don't talk to the person, if you continually talk about his or her problem, if you use threats of eternal damnation, you will make the person build a bigger defense system to hide the sin. Remember that you believe Christ has died to pay for your loved one's sin, even if she or he doesn't see the sin or the forgiveness. Act out your faith. Don't expect sinners to be able to change themselves. It can't be done. Refer them to Christ, who not only forgives but also gives us the power to grow in living by His righteousness rather than our own.

A difference in value systems

Members of the same family will have different opinions about what is, and what is not, a problem because they have different value systems. One member may think it is a problem to move from job to job or from state to state. Another may think it is fun to change jobs and locations often. One may believe it is bad financial planning to have a credit card balance. Another may think it is wise to charge things now because the price might go up.

Some families have open warfare between morning people and night people. Morning people know that it is good to go to bed early, get a good night's sleep, and be up before the sun each morning. (They phone other family members at 7 A.M.) Others don't function well until after lunch. They do their best thinking, studying, and work after the evening news and the late-night shows. (They call other family members at 10:30 P.M.) Follow the motto, "Different strokes for different folks," and don't let the differences in your family give you a stroke.

One's living schedule is not a problem as long as one has one. But a family needs an understanding of different ways of life. What is the right way for one is a problem for another.

"When we were first married, I lived a thousand miles from my husband's family, and I loved them. Then we moved back near all my in-laws. Every one of them felt free to walk into our house at any time they wanted. I couldn't believe it. I'd go to the kitchen and find a brother-in-law eating cookies I planned for dinner. I complained to my husband, but he seemed to think it was normal. I think it's weird."

The point for you: Understand that what you consider a problem may not be a problem for others in your family. Learn to identify the differences in value systems and find a way to accept one another's differences without forcing everyone to accept yours. And keep your value system without being forced to do things that are uncomfortable for you. The best advice on this one: Learn to laugh about it. Strange relatives will give you something interesting to talk about.

A difference in experiences

Even though members of a family may be very close and share most of the experiences of their lives, each will have unique experiences that affect him or her in a way that can cause problems.

For example: Those who have been through financial depressions, wars, serious health problems, or unemployment will view many parts of life from a different perspective than those who have only heard about such things. Those who have had more education will have a different view than those who haven't.

Each one's job will give a different view of life. Attend a family reunion that includes members of a labor union and those who work in management to get a good idea of how experiences influence our views of life. Those who grew up with a religious faith will have a different view than those who have no faith or those who became involved in faith later in life.

"I love to go back to the house and neighborhood where I grew up. It was a happy childhood for me. I couldn't understand why my sister, only a few years younger, had such a different view of the same place. We were a happy family and had good times together. When we were adults, my sister finally told me how she was sexually harassed by an old man in the neighborhood. She had a different view. I had hiding places for fun—good memories. She had hiding places for fear—bad memories. Since she told me about those problems, I no longer push for family reunions back in the old neighborhood."

"I was seriously ill as a child. The sickness and its aftereffects lasted about three years. After I was married, my wife helped me see that my relationship with my parents was different than how my siblings related to them. Because of the sickness, my parents treated me differently. My brothers and sisters had more conflicts with them than I did. Once I became aware of that, I understood my brothers and sisters a lot better."

Many families continue to live with the same misunderstandings and problems year after year. They are like a person who has a rock in his shoe but who doesn't stop to remove the rock. If you see the same struggle repeated in your family, take a look at yourself and others. It could be that you are making problems for others about issues that could be resolved. Or maybe you are making more problems about an issue that you and others could live with if you stayed out of the situation. Start by understanding that you may have a different definition of the problem.

A difference in expectations

Some problems do not start with the individual and spread to the family. Instead, the family creates the problem for the individual. For example, an adult son is happy with his work but his parents want him to do something else. The parents have the problem and they create a problem about their problem if they try to talk their son into a different career. Their second problem is a strain, or even a fracture, in their relationship with their son.

"I like being a mechanic. My favorite Christmas was when my older brother got an Erector Set that he didn't play with. I played with it all the time. But my parents wanted me to go into church work. Sometimes they dropped hints, sometimes they gave advice, sometimes they tried to tell me what to do. I like being a mechanic, but they have made it a problem for me."

Some adult sons and daughters will expect things from their parents that the parents cannot, or will not, give. They may want their parents to have a different home or to change their style of living. They may expect parents to take vacations to places and at times that please the sons and daughters. The variety of different expectations between parents and their adult offspring is limitless.

The point for you: Instead of dealing with the problems created by the problem of different expectations, take the time to discover the real problem. Recognize that different expectations always will cause conflict. It will be easier to accept and live with the different expectations than to struggle with the problems caused by the problem.

Whose Problem Is It?

Problems always belong to "them." Whether it is government, church, community, or family, "they" cause the problem. Listen to others talk about problems and notice how easy it is to discuss things that are wrong—as long as others are responsible. Then admit that you do it too.

When family members talk about problems, they most often see those caused by others. There are so many stories about family members who think their every problem is caused by others in the family that I will not use any of them here. Many have been, or will be, used in other parts of this book. Instead, I am going to give two overdone characterizations of the view from two different generations. Please understand that, as in a cartoon, I am exaggerating certain attitudes to illustrate a point. In most families the difference is more subtle—but it is there.

A member of Generation B says

"I have given my life for my children, and what do I get for it? I slaved to support them. I never got the things I wanted for myself because I always gave everything to my children. Now I'm the one in need, and they won't help me. I'm in poor health because I took care of them instead of myself. I'm poor because I spent all my money on them. I'm lonely because I spent my time on them and their friends instead of making friends for myself. They don't care. They've got no time for me now. I gave my life for them, and they've given me nothing."

A member of Generation C says

"I'm 35 years old and my parents still try to run my life as though I were only 10. They don't approve of my job or my spouse. They don't think I'm raising my kids right—as though they were such a good example. They bring up every mistake I made since they had to change my diapers. Even when they don't say anything, I feel their criticism. They've messed with my head so much that I don't know who I am."

The answer to both generations is: *Get a life!*

It's your fault I have problems

One of the major problems about a problem is the cop-out excuse, "It's your fault that I have problems." Many people blame the government, society, God, the church, or the boss for their problems. But the chief target is members of the family.

Blaming someone else for your problem creates a new problem because it prevents you from dealing with the issues. If the problem is caused by someone else, it must be solved by someone else. Therefore, when you blame others, you excuse yourself from responsibility. The fact is that you cannot change others, but you can change yourself.

Even in situations where the other generation did cause the problems, you will not help yourself deal with the issue by continuing to blame other family members. Part of your need to define your life is to accept the fact that your children have hurt the family and, therefore, have hurt you. And your children also feel that you have hurt them. The challenge is not to convince everyone else how badly you were treated but to deal with the reality in a way that will not destroy you. Accept the fact that you have a problem caused by other family members and do not make more problems by continuing the struggle. Again, let's look at extremes.

Maybe your adult children were abused physically, mentally, or sexually by you, your spouse, or someone else. Maybe your divorce solved your problems but created problems for your children. Maybe you spent too much time at work or on your hobby, or your social life took precedence over your children. It will not help your adult sons or daughters to find you guilty either in the courts of law or the courts of public opinion. You know you failed them. They know it too. But that's not a reason for them to be failures. Your adult children need to look for the good things you did and maintain a limited relationship based on those positive parts. Find help from a counselor, from God, or from other family members and friends so you can be lifted above the problems you have caused your adult children. Each of you will need to accept the emotional scars as many people accept physical disabilities. Encourage one another to see what can be done with your lives despite the difficulties.

> *"I am the oldest kid in my family. I remember seeing my dad beat up my mother and my sisters. I saw him drunk, and I knew he was unfaithful to my mother before I was old enough to even know what sex is. For years I hated him. I was glad my parents got a divorce, even though we lived in poverty. I made something of my life. I feel good about my job, my marriage, and my kids. My father-in-law is the father I never had. When I got my own life together, a strange thing happened. I don't hate my dad anymore. I can write to him and talk to him on the phone. I can pray for him. He has not ruined my life."*

Your children may not have followed the example you gave them. They may have rejected your advice, your faith, even you. They may have cheated you out of money, caused tensions between you and your spouse, embarrassed you before your extended family and friends. On top of all that, they may blame you for everything they have done wrong. If you accept all that guilt, your life will be ruined. You already hurt because your adult sons and daughters have problems. If you add the extra problem that it is all your fault, you will never be able to help them deal with their issues. You were not a perfect parent—no one has been. Apologize for the mistakes you did make. Ask forgiveness from your family and from God. Then go on with your life and do not whip yourself for your children's misbehavior. Remember that you have other parts of your life to lead. Build your life on other good relationships in your family, on friends, and on other relationships and activities that help you understand who you are.

> *"My son is 38 years old and a college graduate. He has never held a job for more than two years. Thank God he has never married. He asks me for money. Now he is living on welfare. In our last phone conversation, he asked me if I had any goals in my life and went on to explain how my life seemed worthless to him."*

Suggestions

- Recognize your problems. Do not blame them on others. If others are involved, you may need to ask them for help. But ask them to help you with your problem rather than putting the blame on them. If they say they don't have a problem (when you think they do), accept their view but explain your problem and ask for their help.

"I think my father is an alcoholic. He doesn't agree. As long as we argued about whether he was an alcoholic, we couldn't stand to be in the same room. I was always looking for a way to find him guilty, and he was always looking for a way to show that he could drink and have no problem. So I backed off. I explained to him that I had a problem. My problem was that I hurt because I thought he was hurting himself. I explained that I would deal with my problem. I went to Al-Anon and got help. Since then he drinks a lot less around me. Maybe that is not solving what I perceive to be his problem, but it has helped me. And I know I am doing more to help him now than when we argued all the time."

• Remember that when you accuse someone else of being wrong, that person's natural reaction is to put up a defense. If someone in your family blames you, try not to defend yourself. Remember the other person loves you. Maybe that loved one has not used the best methods to talk about the problem, but try to look beyond the tactics and see the love. When you want to talk to a member of your family about

his or her problem, speak of it as a problem
that can be helped rather than a fault that must
be condemned.

- Deal with the real issues. I say it one more time:
Don't make problems about the problems.

That's Not My Problem

Problems often come in pairs that are opposite
extremes. One extreme of a family problem is to say,
"It's your fault that I have problems," and blame
everything on someone else. The opposite extreme is
to react to things that hurt other family members by
saying, "That's not my problem." I learned long ago
that I cannot be right all the time, but I can avoid
extremes. God gives us a promise through Isaiah that
helps me: "The Lord will make you go through hard
times, but He Himself will be there to teach you, and
you will not have to search for Him any more. If you
wander off the road to the right or the left, you will
hear His voice behind you saying, 'Here is the road.
Follow it' " (Isaiah 30:20–21).

You go off one side of the road if you blame all
your problems on others in your family—or if you let
other family members put the blame for all their
problems on you.

You go off the other side of the road if you refuse
to help other family members by saying that you are
not involved. Likewise, you also go off if you think
you have to handle all your problems alone and not
let members of your family help you.

Accept God's promise that He will say to you, "Here is the road. Follow it." Look for the middle of the road that allows you to be involved with the problems that hurt other members of your family without arguing about whose fault it is. Also be willing to let others help you without pulling them down with you.

One of the most difficult decisions is to know when to give help to others and when to let others handle their problem. The other side is to know when to ask for help and when to insist on taking care of yourself. God defines the ditch on either side of the road and helps us stay on track. "Help carry one another's burdens, and in this way you will obey the law of Christ" (Galatians 6:2). Three verses later: "For everyone has to carry his own load" (verse 5).

"I had been away from my parents' home for 12 years when I got a divorce. It made sense for my ex-wife to keep the house. I was short on money. I didn't feel right about asking my parents if I could live with them, but they invited me. We talked about it, and I moved back into my old bedroom. It was the best thing that could have happened to me. I needed their emotional support and they needed to know that I wasn't adding more problems to my life."

"My husband and I agreed not to give our 38-year-old son any more money. He showed no responsibility in taking care of himself because he knew we would bail him out. Then I found out that

*he would be living in a shelter for homeless people.
So I would send him twenty dollars at a time to
keep him one step above being homeless. Then I
realized that he may have been using the shelter
story to get the money. Even if it were true, it
meant he had to live in a public shelter before he
would accept responsibility to provide for himself."*

The statement, "It's not my problem," can have
two different effects on the person who is hurting. It
can say, "You're responsible for yourself. Do something about it." Or it can say, "I can't help you." Just
as in some cases it is better to let your adult son or
daughter solve his or her own problems, there may
be times when you are unable to help because you
have your own difficulties.

*"My daughter used her kids to blackmail me. If
I didn't give her money, she would deprive the children of something and blame me. She forged my
name on checks, and I knew that if I didn't make the
check good, she would go to jail and her children
would be put in foster care. At first, I let her control
me. But I had to face the fact that I was not helping
her. One of the most difficult things I have ever
done is to refuse to bail her out one more time."*

Some suggestions

- Could it be that one of your adult children needs
  your help but is afraid to admit to a problem and

ask for help? Do you need to be more open and available to members of your family?

"If my Dad could just hug me one time and tell me that he loves me, I could handle the other struggles I have in life. I'm sure he loves me, but I need that assurance to come from him, not from myself."

- Do you need to ask your adult offspring for help? Do you feel pain because they don't offer to help you when they don't know what you need? If you have asked them for help and they didn't respond, could it be that you were too vague in explaining your problem?

"I thought my parents would disown me if they found out that I had been arrested for shoplifting. I couldn't tell them about the compulsion that makes me do something that I hate. But I knew it would be worse if they read about my arrest in the paper, so I told them. I was surprised how they reacted. They cried and hugged me. They said they would help me get counseling. I'm so glad I told them."

- Be aware of your limitations. If you are helping a family member through a crisis and find yourself being pulled down emotionally or physically, get help for yourself. You can't give strength that you don't have. It may be easier for you to go to a counselor, pastor, or other caregiver than for the hurting person in your family to ask for help. By asking for help for yourself, you may open the way for your loved one to ask for help also.

Must the Problem Be Solved?

Most of us want a quick fix for ourselves and for others. If we are sick, the doctor will take care of it. A lawyer should solve every legal problem. A counselor should solve all emotional stress. And God can take care of the rest.

But real life doesn't always work that way. In many situations the solution is not to eliminate the problem but to find a way to live with it without letting it destroy you. Many times God answers our prayers, not by doing what we want but by giving us the faith to endure and to do what He wants.

There comes a time when we accept our own problems and those of our loved ones. We accept limitations and differences. We accept failures and disappointments. We even accept them though they may continue to do wrong things.

In some cases we will have to put limits on the relationship between parents and adult sons and daughters. But the limited relationship is better than no relationship at all.

One more time: You have problems. Other members of your family have problems. Live with those realities, but don't make problems about the problems.

8
Faith That Unites, Faith That Divides

By now you have figured out why this is not a "how to" book. The "how to" system teaches tactics and methods—a good way to learn how to reupholster sofas and balance your checkbook on the computer. But to look for tactics and methods to get along with your adult sons and daughters, and to help them get along with you, could increase rather than decrease struggles in your family. If other family members have learned different tactics and methods, you will develop another one of those problems-about-the-problem discussed in the previous chapter.

Instead of being a "how to" book this is a "Who is" book. It is concerned about your definitions of parent and adult son or daughter—and other relationships that affect those two. It is concerned about those who are involved in your life and those who feel that you are involved in their lives.

God is among those who are involved in your life and in the lives of others in your family. God also made it His business to be involved in our lives. Even those who are not part of a church or any spiritual activities have gods that they serve—and, therefore, have gods that they believe will protect and provide for them. These gods become part of the way individuals and families make decisions. When family members share a religious faith, that experience can be one of the most defining parts of their relationship. When they have different religious convictions, it can be one of the most dividing issues in their lives.

God Who Became Human and Remained God

This book was planned, written, and published by people who believe that Jesus Christ is God who became human so He could be our Savior. We do not have a choice of gods from which we make a selection. We have a God who has found us. Therefore, this book is offered to those who believe in Jesus Christ and to those who are struggling in life—those who need the help that Jesus gives us, not only in families but also as individuals. It is also offered to those who feel the pain of family struggles and are seeking help. The message to them is that Christ has come to help them in their need.

Previously, I have mentioned that the book is for those who are Christians and those who want Christian values. Christian values are part of the "how to" idea. They teach how to live the good life and how to live with yourself and others. Being a Christian is part of the "Who is" book you are reading. It is about who you are—a sinner who causes problems for others and lives with other sinners who cause problems for you. It is about who Jesus is. He is your Savior who has forgiven your sins, and He is also the Savior of all other members of your family. He has forgiven their sins—even those sins that have caused you so much trouble that you are reading this book.

The "how to" of religion is what divides people from one another. The issues—how to worship God, how to serve God, how to be a moral person, how to live with other people who have a different "how to" book—always cause religious debates in families and have caused religious wars among nations.

The "Who is" issues unite us. Who is a sinner? We all are.

> As the Scriptures say: "There is no one who is righteous, no one who is wise or who worships God. All have turned away from God; they have all gone wrong; no one does what is right, not even one." (Romans 3:10–12)

> There is no difference at all: everyone has sinned and is far away from God's saving presence. (Romans 3:22–23)

Our common sinfulness removes all the debates about who is right and who is wrong. It makes us know we all need help. When we know our own sinfulness, we look at the sins of others in a different light. We can't solve the problems of other family members, but we can refer them to the One who has forgiven us.

That brings us to the next part of the "Who is" approach to problems. Jesus is the Savior of us all. He has died to pay for all guilt. He has risen from the dead to give everyone eternal life. "But by the free gift of God's grace all are put right with Him through Christ Jesus, who sets them free" (Romans 3:24).

You are a different person because you believe in Jesus Christ. Your faith changes the answer to the question, "Who are you?" In Christ you are a new person—a saint made holy by the righteousness of Christ. That new you then affects the way you see the others in your family and how you answer the question, "Who are they?" Whether they believe it (an issue to be discussed later), Christ has paid for their sin. Your relationship with others no longer is based on "how to" (as you tell them how to solve their problems—and thereby your own). Instead it is based on "Who is" as you tell them who Jesus is and how that changes who they are.

Jesus' goal in life was to remove the things that divide us and to bring us together with Him so we also could be united with one another.

> *[Jesus said,] "I pray that they may all be one. Father! May they be in us, just as You are in Me and I am in You. May they be one, so that the world will believe that You sent Me. I gave them the same glory You gave Me, so that they may be one, just as You and I are one. I in them and You in Me, ... in order that the world may know that You sent Me and that You love them as You love Me." (John 17:21–23)*

Now to deal with the paradox. People who are united by principles (how to) also are divided from those who have different principles. The same issues that unite them with some will divide them from others. It is also true that those who are united by relationships (Who is) are divided by those who do not share in that relationship. Christian faith unites families. Christian faith divides families. Jesus knew that. He said:

> *"Do not think that I have come to bring peace to the world. No, I did not come to bring peace, but a sword. I came to set sons against their fathers, daughters against their mothers, daughters-in-law against their mothers-in-law; a man's worst enemies will be the members of his own family. Whoever loves his father or mother more than Me is not fit to be My disciple; whoever loves his son or daughter more than Me is not fit to be My disciple." (Matthew 10:34–37)*

If members of your family believe in Jesus Christ as Lord and Savior, you have a great resource to help you deal with problems that divide. You have a mutual relationship with a Savior who wants to bring you together. This chapter reminds you of that fact. Use the gifts that God has given to you and to other members of your family as a strength to help you. Worship together, if not in the same place, then in the same Spirit. As you confess your sins, be aware that others in your family also are confessing theirs. As you are told you are forgiven by Christ, remember that others receive that same forgiveness. Be aware that you and others in your family are baptized into union with Jesus Christ; therefore, since you are united with Him you also are united with one another. As you discuss different teachings, remember that you are discussing varying doctrines—not rejecting one another's Christianity. Remember:

> *The cup we use in the Lord's Supper and for which we give thanks to God: when we drink from it, we are sharing in the blood of Christ. And the bread we break: when we eat it, we are sharing in the body of Christ. Because there is the one loaf of bread, all of us, though many, are one body, for we all share the same loaf. (1 Corinthians 10:16–17)*

What if the members of your family do not share the Christian faith or do not share an understanding of the Christian faith? Jesus knew that would happen. He told us we would be divided by our faith in Him. However, that does not mean your faith in Christ is not a resource to help you in your fractured family. The one who believes still has the powerful energy of the Gospel of Christ to use for oneself and for others in the family.

When Some Do Not Believe in Christ

First, let's consider the problem in a family divided because some are Christian and others are not. (Even if this is not true in your family, pay close attention to this section. Some people do not recognize the resource they have in their Christian faith to help them deal with family problems. An awareness of what it would be like to not share faith in Christ can help you make more use of the faith you have.)

Perhaps the most common situation is a family where the children were baptized, raised on Sunday school and church activities, confirmed—and then left their faith. This can cause the parents to blame themselves, the church, and their adult sons and daughters.

> *"The biggest sorrow in our lives is that our son and his family will not go to church with us or even pray with us. We wouldn't care if they went to another Christian denomination, but they have joined what we regard as a cult. They talk about Jesus, but do not see Him as our Lord and Savior. We worry about our grandchildren because they are not baptized and are not getting a Christian education."*

In other cases parents have become Christians after their children left home. The children feel betrayed because their parents defected from unbelief.

> *"When our last child left home, we sold our house and moved to a smaller one. Our new neighbors invited us to church. We went because we wanted to make new friends, even though we had no interest in religion. We soon discovered that our idea about religion and faith in Jesus Christ were*

two very different things. We found great joy in our faith. Our kids thought we had gone nuts. They suspected we were getting senile (at age 45) and said we were just afraid to die so we were grabbing at religion."

"When I was growing up, my mother and grandmother made me go to church. My father tolerated it, but I could tell that he thought it was silly. We had little secret jokes about religion. He never went to church and I didn't either once I left home. When I came back for Christmas one year, I was shocked to find that my father had joined the church and really gotten involved. I felt betrayed. Now he believes and I don't."

Families that include those who believe in Christ and those who don't soon realize how faith is a part of everyday life. They may agree not to talk about religion, but faith is more than talking. Do the believing members still have mealtime prayers when the nonbelievers are guests in their home? If the believing one is a guest in the other's home, does he sneak a silent prayer in? Can you celebrate Christmas together? It may be hard to plan family activities when one individual considers Sunday a time to worship and another thinks of it as activity time. Will Christian parents want to leave money in their wills to heirs who might give it to a non-Christian religion? Who makes funeral arrangements?

"My wife and I come from two very different families. I had a brother who had not been in a church since he was 10—and that was because our grandmother invited us to dinner on condition we go to church. When he died, his children, who had become Christians, had a big church funeral for him. I was afraid he was going to jump out of the casket. Meanwhile, my wife had a sister who was one of those in-church-six-days-a-week people. She always said she was making up for those who only went once a week. When she died, her kids refused to plan a funeral—just out-to-the-cemetery-and-into-the-ground. Not even a prayer."

The moral of the story is: Plan your own funeral according to the faith you do or don't have.

Jesus was right when He said that He would be a cause for division (Matthew 10:34–36). His words state that a man's worst enemies would be the members of his own family. Remember, the same Jesus said, "But I tell you: love your enemies and pray for those who persecute you" (Matthew 5:44).

As I write this, I assume that the family members who are Christian are the ones reading my words. If I am wrong, then please mark this section and give it to the Christian members of your family.

To those who are Christian: Your faith in Christ helps you hear Scripture in a way that unbelievers cannot. You know that Christ has died to forgive your sins and to help you live by His power. His action on the cross not only forgives your past but also changes your future. Another person may regard you as an enemy because you believe in Christ—but because you believe in Christ, you love that person who sees you as an enemy.

Too often people use the Bible to tell other people what to do rather than hear it as God telling them what to do. For example: As I write this, a man stands on a corner near my office with a cardboard sign that tells me that if I feed him, I am feeding Jesus. That is a quote from Matthew 25:40. However, that quote from Jesus was not given so I can tell others to provide for me. It was given so I can live out my faith by providing for others. The Bible does not tell me to tell you to forgive me. Instead, it tells me that Christ has forgiven me and I can forgive others.

Application for your family: If you are the Christian in a split-family situation, then Jesus' words, "Love your enemies," are spoken to you—not to the members of your family who do not believe in Him. Jesus has loved you; now it's your turn to do the loving. "We were God's enemies, but He made us His friends through the death of His Son. Now that we are God's friends, how much more will we be saved by Christ's life!" (Romans 5:10)

Others in our family may be angry at us because of our faith and because we insist on living our faith. But part of living that faith (maybe the most important part for you at this time) is to follow the system Jesus used for dealing with enemies. He loved us and thereby made us His friends. We love those who object to our faith and thereby make them our friends.

We believe that Christ has died for all sins. That means He has not only forgiven you, He also has forgiven those members of your family who do not believe in Him. Granted, if they do not believe, they do not know that their sins are forgiven. But the point is that you know. Do you treat those who do not believe as though you believe that Christ is also their Savior? Do you know it is not your job to punish them for their sins but instead to show them (you may even have to use words) that Christ has already taken their punishment?

> *"I've always prayed for my children—for their protection, health, tests, ball games, and all the other things that parents pray for. Now they are all adults. I'm not sure that one of them still believes in Christ. In fact, my son told me he doesn't pray anymore. I still pray for him, and I've found something new in the phrase 'pray for.' I pray for him in his place. He does not thank God for his family, health, and job—so I do it for him. He doesn't ask for spiritual guidance—so I do it for him. I think that is part of what it means to be a priesthood of believers. Like priests, we pray not just for ourselves but for others. One thing I pray for is that my son will again do his own praying."*

When Jesus tells us that faith in Him will cause divisions in our families, He is not telling us to do the dividing. Instead, we are to recognize the divisive issue. It is true that our faith is the cause of a division, but that same faith is also the gift that gives unity. And we who believe are the ones who get to practice our faith.

When Our Faith in Christ Has Different Results

When some members of a family believe in Christ and others don't, the division is obvious. The separation is a faith issue. One believes in Christ. One believes in another god or does not believe at all—which is still a faith issue. Other families have a different problem that causes divisions. They may all believe that Jesus Christ is their Lord and Savior, but their faith has different results in their lives.

When it's a matter of commitment

Sometimes the differences are caused by a different understanding of commitment. Because of their faith, some attend church services regularly, have family devotions, give time and money to the church, and speak of their faith. Others in the same family may belong to the same denomination and the same congregation. However, they feel that their faith is a personal, even private, thing. They go to church now and then, decline all requests to sing in the choir or to teach Sunday school, and give from whatever they happen to have in their billfold on the day they happen to be in church. A family that includes members with such different attitudes may not enjoy the faith they share.

*"The only way I can get my sons and their fam-
ilies to church is to invite them to Sunday dinner
and insist they meet me there. My grandchildren
would not be in Sunday school if I didn't take them.
When my husband died, I know they got great comfort in the faith he had taught them. I asked my son
if his children would know that he had a faith like
their grandfather's. He got upset at me and told me
that, just as we were responsible for raising him, he
was responsible for his children."*

*"I can't understand why my mother is always
on my case about going to church. She is the one
who makes the big deal about Jesus loving all of us
and that we don't have to earn His love. Yet she
sounds as though He takes attendance at church
and charges admission. I believe in Jesus, and I
want my kids to do the same. Isn't that enough?"*

For the record: In some cases the stories are
reversed. Members of Generation C are deeply
involved in their church, and their parents are drop-ins.

Again the responsibility for applying the Christian faith to family problems falls on the one who
makes an issue of it. If you are the one who has commitments to serve Christ in worship, stewardship of
time and money, and by your personal witness, be
aware that it is a blessing from God that you can do
such things. You are not doing such things *to earn* salvation, you are doing them *because Christ has given
you* salvation. It is a privilege to serve God. Be thank-

ful that you have that privilege. The best way to encourage your adult sons and daughters, or your parents, to join you in your commitment to Christ is to enjoy your Christian ministry. Tom Sawyer proved that if you think it is fun to paint a fence, your friends will want to help. If you love serving Jesus, others who see your love will be influenced by it.

On the other hand, if someone in the family complains because others are too involved in church life, that person is making the issue and, therefore, must defend his or her own level of involvement on the basis of the faith professed. Do not try to take away the joy a family member has in living out the Christian faith. Strange as it may sound, many who complain because religion was pushed on them will try to pull others away from an active faith.

> *"We have accepted the fact that our two children do not want to be involved in church life the way we do, and we do not nag them about it. But we do resent their efforts to interfere in our faith life. They make remarks about our being too 'churchy.' They plan things for us to be with our grandchildren on Sunday mornings. I know they resent the fact that we have included the church in our will."*

Now if you are the family member who believes in Jesus but does not want to overdo the religious stuff (you have been identified as that person if a family member has given you this book with this paragraph underlined): Please do not be offended that your adult son or daughter is on your case. Don't let their pushiness become an excuse for not becoming more involved in your faith.

Remember that they talk about spiritual issues with you because they love you. Their tactics may irk you—and may even contradict the very idea of God's grace that they want to share with you. But remember this is not a "how to" book. Ignore their methods and think about the relationship you have with your family. That is the "Who is" part. Accept the love that they offer to you, but don't fake a faith to please them.

Next, ask yourself if you have developed a spiritual dependence on another family member. Understand the concept "spiritual dependence" by comparing it to financial dependence. Sometimes one family member will bail out anyone else who gets into financial problems. After a while the other members of the family don't worry about bills. They know the "rich one" will keep them from going bankrupt. Similarly, some families have one person who becomes the spiritually "rich one." Other family members expect that one to do the church things. The one who has the church connection keeps the others on the membership roles; arranges baptisms, weddings, and funerals; and in general conducts the spiritual business of the family.

Do you expect someone else in your family to be the faithful one for you? Is your connection to Christ through another person's faith? If so, that means you have an in-law or a step-relationship with God.

Maybe it is time for you to become spiritually independent from family members and accept your responsibility for a living relationship with Christ.

> *"Let me tell you about a strange thing that happened in my family. Aunt Agnes was a churchgoer. She was there every Sunday for both worship and Bible class. If a job had to be done at church, she would do it or find someone else who would. The family felt that Aunt Agnes gave too much money to the church. She had one daughter, Carol, who never went to church. It was the sorrow of Aunt Agnes' life. When my aunt died, Carol went to church for the funeral and hasn't stopped since. She is involved in church almost, not quite, like her mother. It seemed that she finally grew up spiritually."*

Be grateful for the faith you do share and use it to help all members of the family to be more spiritual people. That works best when faith is a joy, not an obligation or a cause for constant criticism.

When it's a matter of different methods

Faith is a personal thing because it reaches to the soul—the very core of our lives. We all have deep spiritual feelings that are often hard to express but are very important to us. Many times, these deep feelings become connected with outward forms of worship that are more visible and, therefore, more easily discussed. However, these outward methods sometimes will hide or even impair the deep feelings we have. Members of a family who belong to the same Christian denomination and, in some cases, even the same congregation, may be divided on the methods of worship and service in the church.

"When our son and his family moved to another state, we were delighted that they found a congregation in our denomination. They became much more involved than they had been in our home church. But when we visited them, we were shocked! They sang songs (I don't think they were hymns) out of a different book. The order of service was different. They called the pastor by his first name. It didn't seem like church to us."

Look at the two extremes: In some churches people kneel when they pray and often criticize those who pray with hands held high. In other churches people pray with hands held high and often criticize those who kneel to pray. Is there a lesson in those extremes for you and your family? Is your unity in Christ or in ritual? In some families the spiritual unity can be assumed because the ritual is the same. Maybe it is a blessing to have some differences in methods in your family because you will need to discuss the differences and discover the real unity in Christ.

Other families find themselves divided because they see their faith from different points of view. Some members of the family proclaim that Christ is the Savior of all, and others want to announce who is going to hell and why.

"We were so glad when our daughter moved back to our area and belonged to our church again. But something had happened to her. She had become critical of all other Christians. She seems to have a negative faith and rarely shows the joy of being with other Christians. Instead she points out how everyone else is wrong in what they teach and what they do. Her faith seems to have moved from her heart to her head."

Christians regard themselves as a family and often think of one another as brothers and sisters in Christ. Sometimes they misunderstand the concept of the Christian family and think that its hometown is the Garden of Eden. In reality we are a spiritual family with all the dysfunctions that are part of human families. There is sibling rivalry, even in the Christian family.

Sometimes members of a family will not get the same results from the same experience.

"Soon after our son was confirmed, we moved. He became withdrawn from us and hid himself in sports. When we had conversations, my voice was the only one I heard. After several months, he broke down and cried one night when I suggested we pray together. His confirmation experience had been awful for him, even though for years his dad had built up confirmation as a meaningful part of his youth. I had to say that parents are not always right and that pastors could be wrong too. We had

*to help our son see the difference between the faith
taught and the method used to teach it."*

One member of Generation B asked that this
book include her message to both generations:

> *"The only path to peace is forgiveness—honest
> and true forgiveness, the kind Christ gives to us.
> Please, in some way make it clear to your readers
> that forgiveness—plain, humble, unconditional
> forgiveness—is so beautiful and so healing."*

The members of the family who go to the source
of their faith and give to others what they have
received from Christ will create unity. Those who go
to the edge of their faith to find fault and condemn
others will continue the process of division.

When it's a matter of different denominations

The Christian family is divided into sub-families
of denominations. This division did not start at the
Reformation. Already in New Testament times, titles
that indicated separation were given the unifying
name "Christian." There were Jewish Christians and
Greek Christians; they had different histories and different views. There was the Christian church in Anti-
och and the Christian church in Jerusalem and the
Christian church in Corinth. All had the same Gospel,
but each had its own culture and the need to minister
to that culture.

Today's families are part of the "split heirs" of all
the old divisions. More than ever before, members of

Generation C belong to different denominations than their parents. This phenomenon will increase because it means that more than ever before members of Generation D will grow up in a family with parents from two different denominations. Are members of your family united by a faith in Christ and divided by denominational differences?

Start with the most important issue: Do you believe that your loved one is still in the Christian faith and will be with you in heaven because Jesus Christ is his or her Savior? If you can say yes to that question, you have a powerful bond between you that holds you together now as well as in the future.

Next, what are the issues that divide you? Do you disagree on important issues, such as who Jesus is and what He has done for us? Do you have different opinions about the purpose and blessing of Baptism and the Lord's Supper? Do you have a different view of the Holy Scripture? Do you have a different understanding of the work of the Holy Spirit? Do some of you believe that God has found you, and others believe they have found God?

These are all important issues (for those who have certain views of them) because these teachings give us the assurance of our salvation and the power to share the Gospel of Christ with others. Now an important point: Not only would people from different denominations have different answers on the issues in the previous paragraph, they also would ask different questions. To some Baptism and the Lord's Supper are not important issues and are ignored because discussions about them might cause division. To others they are gifts from God that are treasures; to ignore them is to ignore a gift Christ gave. To some the Holy Spirit is the "Holy Who?" and to others the Holy Spirit overshadows Christ rather than reveals Him.

Even listing these issues can cause division, but to ignore them can result in unity based on nonfaith rather than on faith. So what is a family to do when they belong to different Christian denominations?

First, recognize the unity you do have in Christ. Turn the lemon into lemonade by using the problem as an opportunity to discuss the foundation of your faith.

> *"I was worried about my parents' reaction when I told them I was joining my wife's church. But I was surprised. They said they were glad that I had married a Christian, even if she was from a different denomination. I know they don't like some of the details of the differences, but in some ways we are closer spiritually because at least I am back in a church."*

Next, make sure you do not overstate denominational difference. In their zeal to teach the truth of Scripture, some teachers will use a negative method of teaching by pointing out the false teachings of others. We must reject false doctrine, but sometimes the negative method of teaching misrepresents the other denomination's doctrine. Rather than let your family issues be settled by theologians and the powers-that-be in the denominations involved, talk to one another about your faith. Go to the Scripture as a resource rather than to literature that is written to find fault.

Finally, build up your faith, not as a wall that proves you are right but as a power that shares the love of Christ. If you become angry and condemn others, you are not getting the message of Christian love. Check out 1 Corinthians 13 as a resource for discussing the faith you share. The idea of shunning another Christian does not fit the life of one who follows Christ. Follow the plan God has given. We love Him because He first loved us.

Our way of sharing His love with others is to first love them—and to let them love us.

St. Paul's description of the church as the body of Christ also applies to a family: "If one part of the body [family] suffers, all the other parts suffer with it; if one part is praised, all the other parts share its happiness" (1 Corinthians 12:26).

The faith that divides leads away from Christ. The faith that unites depends on Christ for unity.

9
 Defining Moments

The stories told throughout this book are often defining moments in the lives of the people who told the stories. Each of us have moments in our lives when we learn something, understand something that we already knew, or get some other new insight into ourselves or other people. Such events help us understand ourselves, and we often tell the stories to explain ourselves to others. We also learn to understand others when we see or hear something in another person's life that helps us know more about him or her.

For you and the other members of your family to make the most of your relationships, you need to know and to share the defining moments of your lives. Each chapter of this book has asked the questions and told the stories to help you understand yourself and others in your family. You and others in your family may need a counselor or a pastor to help you sort out the tangled relationships that often develop among near-relatives. But eventually the job is yours. You need to know yourself and your need to want a loving relationship with your adult sons and daughters. And you need to help them have such a relationship with you. Look for the defining moments that have united you and for those that divide you.

The Rituals of Life

Many defining moments are connected with the big events that we celebrate on a certain day but are part of our entire lives. For a complete list of such events, look at the greeting card store in your local shopping mall. How many of the cards remind you of big events in your family?

- *Baptisms* are times when many families are together for worship and for a party. The event recognizes the spiritual heritage the family shares with the newest family member. It also shows the family commitment to a continued spiritual relationship together. It is a time for those who may have forgotten the spiritual meaning of Baptism but remembered the ritual to check their roots and think of their own relationship to Christ.

- For many families, *confirmation* celebrates that Christian education has occurred and emphasizes the spiritual commitment made in confirmation vows. The person making the confirmation vows recognizes family support and accepts a responsibility to give that support to others.

- *Graduations*, from kindergarten through graduate school, give families a chance to rejoice in the education one of them has received and a way to encourage the honored guest to continue learning.

- *Weddings* recognize that marriage involves more people than the bride and the groom. The bride and groom's joy will be felt by everyone else who loves them. The pains in their marriage will be felt by the others in the family.

- *Funerals* bring family members together from great distances and across great divisions. A death in the family is a reality check. Can we really help one another when we all need that help?

   "My childhood family of seven spread all over the country. When one brother died, we were all together for the first time since our father's death. Each of us had seen the others, but we hadn't been together. At first we were down on ourselves for being together only at funerals. Then we realized what a blessing we had. Death didn't divide us—it brought us together because we believe we have a future beyond death. It worked for us."

   "My mother died suddenly. She had a heart attack and, within a matter of minutes, went from being a vigorous person to death. My sister couldn't handle it. She wouldn't even go to the funeral. Dad and the rest of us needed her, and we wanted her to need us. But she cut us off."

Some families do not make a big deal about the major milestones of life. This is a family decision, not a society decision. As long as all generations of a family agree that we're all together because we want to be, or we don't need to make a big fuss over such things, there's no problem. But if one member of the family needs everyone present or accounted for but other members do not want to spend the time or money, you will have a problem.

> *"My parents were divorced when I was a kid, but I always saw my father for a couple of weeks during the summer. When I was in high school, the summer visits became less regular because I had other things to do, but Dad was still important to me. I assumed he would be there to walk me down the aisle when I got married—but he wasn't. I guess we don't agree whether he couldn't be there or he wouldn't, but the fact is my stepfather walked me down the aisle."*

These major events in life can be times when families are reunited after long separations, or they can reopen old wounds and build up the walls of separation. Make sure you understand your expectations and those of other family members before you assume that all will see the big event in the same way.

Birthdays, anniversaries, Christmas, and family reunions also provide rituals for families to share their lives together. Some families have traditions that they repeat year after year and find great joy in the ritual because it is something they can count on. However, some members of the family (especially the new ones, like in-laws) may not share the enthusiasm for the ritual. Traditions are important in life, but they must be updated so they continue to provide the results for which they were originally planned.

Some families did not establish rituals for the big ceremonies and dates in their lives. Later they regret their omission. Maybe it's not too late. Just as old traditions must sometimes be changed or discarded, new rituals can be developed. If you feel your family of parents and adult sons and daughters needs a restart, share your ideas with them. Don't do it on your own or you may be the only one who shows up. Maybe the others also would like to share more of their lives. Talk about it and find out.

When a big event becomes a defining moment for all (or at least most) of the members of the family, the moment brings them together and gives them a memory that will continue to be a bond of unity among them.

The Pictures of Life

The family camera records many of the defining moments of life. There is a common ritual shared by many families. An adult son or daughter brings home a boyfriend or girlfriend. Family members recognize that this friend is special and is probably a keeper. The parents get out the pictures, movies, and now, the videos to show the prospective in-law what kind of child his or her sweetheart was. This ritual often is dreaded by members of Generation C, but there is great wisdom in it.

Looking at family pictures helps all generations understand one another. They see again a moment of their history and remember the feelings. The family album records not only how family members looked at the various ages of their lives but also shows attitudes and feelings.

"Shortly after we got engaged, my fiancé and I spent a weekend with his parents. One evening they showed the slides of their family history. I could tell that my fiancé didn't like the idea, but it was helpful to me. I got to see his parents when they were younger. I could see my future husband in his father and mother. Seeing pictures of my fiancé as a child helped me understand something about his moods and his humor. In the pictures I saw happy and fun-loving kids, but I also saw some anger and resentment. It helped me to understand that."

All people are always changing. To understand ourselves and others, we need to know who we were to understand who we are—and who we will be. Many of our defining moments of the past are recorded in pictures. Look at them to learn about yourself—and other members of your family.

Things That Make My Life and Your Life Our Lives

Members of a family are not held together by legal documents or by their genetic code. The unity of a family comes from the experiences they share with one another. Sometimes these experiences are so much a part of a family that members think all other families do the same thing. At other times, a family is aware that they have something special that is only for them.

"Years ago, at some party, I won a booby prize. I don't know whether it was meant to be an ashtray, a candy dish, or a flowerpot. It was a black foot, and it was ugly. One of our sons had just bought a house, so we gave it to him as a housewarming gift. He gave it to his brother for Christmas. A family ritual was established. Various members of the family would find the black foot at their place of work, in the refrigerator at home, or in a pillow slip."

"When we spent a vacation with a married son, we knew ahead of time that they didn't go to church like we did. We had accepted that. As we got in the car to go for a weekend trip with our son and his wife, we were delighted to hear him say, 'Remember how we always prayed before we went on a trip. We still do that. Would you say the prayer, Dad?'"

Sometimes members of Generation C need a time-out from family traditions. If those from Generation B try to force the issues, it only does more to divide the family. However, later in life, members of Generation C often reach back for the rituals of their childhood—especially when Generation D shows up in the family.

"I knew my daughter didn't go to church after she finished college and got a job in a city far from home. I didn't nag her about it, but at the end of every letter, I would add a Bible verse—always one that offered Christ's love and acceptance. Then I worried that she might think that I was pushing religion on her, so I stopped adding the message from the Bible. About six weeks later, her letter to me ended with a P.S.: 'What happened to the Bible verses? I miss them.' "

Listen to the things that you tell others about your family. The things you want to talk about show how you define your family and your relationships with others. Ask yourself: Are my stories positive or negative? Am I always finding fault or blaming other members of my family. Am I showing others how I really feel about my adult sons and daughters?

Next listen to the things that others in your family talk about when you are together. How do they define themselves in relationship to you? Are they secure in your love? What do they need from you? What do they expect from you?

One-way Defining Moments

When members of a family share a defining moment, they are united by its memory. However, if one person experiences a big moment that others do not share, it may become a dividing experience.

"When I was in high school, our family went on a vacation to visit relatives. They made me go along even though I had to miss three important ball games. The rest of the family had a great time. They still talk about it when we are together and show the pictures of that trip. I resented it then— and I resent it now."

The same experience can define a moment of joy and unity for some members of the family and define an experience of pain and division for others. The major problem of one-way defining moments is that one member of the family must "lose" for another member to "win."

"My parents have this thing about celebrating their wedding anniversary. All of us have to be there—not only me and my two sisters but our spouses and our kids. We all are told clearly that if one is not there, it will ruin the party for everyone. I would like to do something to help my parents enjoy their anniversary, but I have to make my family miserable to do it?"

"When my son got married, I wanted the entire family to be there. One of my nephews was on a basketball team that made it to the state finals—the same day as the wedding. We all were proud of him for being on such a good team, and his absence was an honor rather than an omission."

When families have different interests and different schedules, they face decisions about priorities. Does the need of the individual come first and everyone else is allowed to do his or her own thing? Or does the need of the family come first and majority rules? The solution is difficult because it involves both an individual and a group decision. Some attitude adjustments will help. The following guidelines will not solve the problem but may help members of a family find their own solution.

- If some members of the family use guilt or force to get others to follow them, everyone loses. They all may join in the family activity planned, but it will not create family unity, it even may create division.

- If you are the one that gets your way, do something to help the family members who cooperated with you. Show your appreciation. Offer something to recognize their needs.

- If you are the one who goes along with the family plan and sacrifices your plans, don't resent the event and be a wet blanket on the others. Make your choice under the circumstances and don't blame the others.

"I dread our family dinners for holidays and birthdays at my grandparent's home. Every member of the family will be there because they know they will be criticized if they are not. But they don't enjoy one another. It is always 'show time.' I

hate myself for playing the game, but I can't find a way out of it."

Other one-way defining moments are often small incidents noticed by one person but not by others. Something that seems like good humor to some people will be offensive to others. Something that is said as a casual comment by one person may be heard as a major declaration by another.

"I'm embarrassed about my weight. Everyone in my husband's family is thin, even though they eat too much of all the wrong foods. It seemed to me that every time we were together, they told 'fat jokes,' and I felt they were directed at me. I complained to my husband, but he kept telling me that it wasn't personal. I finally got up my nerve and protested the next time it happened. I was surprised: The offending brother-in-law apologized and the rest agreed that it had been in poor taste. Now I am glad I had the nerve to speak up."

Members of a family share a history, finances, homes, food, spiritual life, emotions, sometimes even clothes. They develop their own methods of communication. They have their special ways of treating one another. All these bonds that hold families together require a special sensitivity. They see one another differently than others see them. They have different expectations of one another than they have of others. However, all these special qualities and events that bond a family together also present a risk for division in a family. The bonds also may make them overly critical of one another. They may become overly sensitive about what other members of the family do or say. They become overly proud and overly embarrassed by one another. All this is because they love one another and depend on one another for most of the defining moments of their lives.

Today Is the Defining Moment of Your Future Together

Perhaps you have read this book because you are concerned about your relationship with your adult sons or daughters. If so, you may want to share this book with them. Perhaps you have read this book because you are happy about your relationship with others in your family and want to keep a good thing going. If so, it still might be a good idea to reinforce that good relationship by sharing ideas.

Whatever is happening in your family now, today and its situation will soon be part of your family history. Most families go through ups and downs in their relationships. As you face whatever struggles you may have today, remember that the way you deal with them now will affect your relationship in the future. Things can always change. If your relationships are good now, don't take other members of your family for granted. "Keep on keeping on" in the good times with your family. If things are bad, don't give up. Keep on loving others in your family, even though you have problems.

"My wedding was wonderful in many ways. One special joy came from my wedding that we didn't expect. My uncle and my cousin (his son) hadn't spoken to each other for five years. No one in the family knew what caused the problem. I even wondered if I should invite both of them to the wedding, but I decided that was their problem. They both came to the wedding and reception. They talked to each other and have gotten along fine ever since. We don't know any more about what solved the problem than we did about what caused it. I think of it as their special wedding gift to me."

Don't try to be a perfect parent or a perfect adult child. Deal with the realities of failures and hurts, and use the love and unity you have. If you only pay attention to the problems with one member of your family, you may miss all the good things you have with others. If you think only about the problems you have with one person, you may miss all the good you have with that same family member.

"When our three children were growing up, we used to joke that they seemed to take turns giving us a rough time. It was as though they would have a meeting and one would say, 'It's my turn to hassle Mom and Dad. You two be good for now.' Fortunately, they took turns at the bad kid duty. They do the same thing to us as adults. It seems that we always have one to worry about. We finally told them how we saw what they were doing. One

*laughed and said, 'You two just need to have some-
one to fuss over all the time.' "*

*In the meantime the older son was out in the field. On
his way back, when he came close to the house, he
heard the music and dancing. So he called one of the
servants and asked him, "What's going on?" "Your
brother has come back home," the servant answered,
"and your father has killed the prize calf, because he
got back safe and sound." The older brother was so
angry that he would not go into the house; so his
father came out and begged him to come in. But he
spoke back to his father, "Look, all these years I have
worked for you like a slave, and I have never disobeyed
your orders. What have you given me? Not even a
goat for me to have a feast with my friends! But this
son of yours wasted all your property on prostitutes,
and when he comes back home, you kill the prize calf
for him!" "My son," the father answered, "you are
always here with me, and everything I have is yours.
But we had to celebrate and be happy, because your
brother was dead, but now he is alive; he was lost, but
now he has been found." (Luke 15:25–32)*

All families share the experiences of this father.
There are times when relationships are strained or
even appear to be lost. That is the time to wait, to
refuse to give up hope. There are times when the family comes back together. That is the time to celebrate.
Families go through such cycles. The story isn't over
until we join the unending party in heaven.